IMAGE-BUILDING & MONEY-RAISING

for 'hard-to-sell' groups

by Yasmin Prabhudas

published by THE DIRECTORY OF SOCIAL CHANGE

**Image-Building & Money-Raising
for 'hard-to-sell' groups**

By Yasmin Prabhudas

Additional research by Karina Holly
Published by the Directory of Social Change
Radius Works, Back Lane, London NW3 1HL

British Library Cataloguing-In-Publication Data
A catalogue record for this book is available from
the British Library

ISBN 1 873860 26 9

Designed and typeset by Linda Parker
Printed in Britain by Page Bros., Norwich

CONTENTS

Acknowledgements

The author would like to extend her thanks to all those organisations which contributed towards the production of this guide, by providing information.

Thanks also to all those organisations which took the time to provide details for case studies:

John O'Neill – *Belfast Law Centre*
Barbara Welford – *Birmingham Settlement*
John Price – *Brecon and District Disabled Club*
Elsa Beckett – *Gemma*
Fran Springfield – *Gender Dysphoria Trust*
Hartley Hanley – *Hideaway Youth Centre*
Geoffrey Cox – *Legalise Cannabis Campaign*
Wallis Hunt – *Life Anew Trust*
Shivananda Khan – *Naz Project*
Keith Best and Mark Astarita – *Prisoners Abroad*

We are also grateful to the Information Department at the Scottish Council for Voluntary Organisations, the Scottish Office Voluntary Sector Liaison Unit, the Information Department at the Welsh Council for Voluntary Action, the Information Department at the Northern Ireland Council for Voluntary Action and the Economic and Social Policy and Rural Teams at the National Council for Voluntary Organisations, for their co-operation and help.

FOREWORD

The idea for this book emerged as a result of research undertaken for our HIV/AIDS Funding Guide (see *Useful Publications*, page 119). The guide showed that of the few funders who are prepared to give money to a "controversial" issue such as HIV, the vast majority only support large national organisations and projects concerned with the needs of children with HIV/AIDS. Small local HIV projects and HIV projects specifically for Black and Asian people and lesbians and gay men all fared badly.

You don't have to look very far to see that there are certain causes and certain types of organisation that find the going harder than others when it comes to fundraising. Smaller less well-known organisations often find attracting funding a more difficult task than those larger organisations whose fundraising expertise and marketing techniques are well developed. Small groups lack the resources to carry out these activities with the degree of professionalism of larger organisations and so are frequently trapped in a vicious circle – they are unable to attract the funds because they do not have the resources with which to attract the funds.

Whilst this problem is undoubtedly difficult to overcome, there are always ways in which organisations, no matter how limited their resources, can enhance their profile – and hence their appeal to funders – on a day-to-day level, without running glitzy high-cost publicity campaigns. It is important that "hard-to-sell" groups recognise that enhancing their public profile is worth investing in and that this, along with an effective fundraising strategy, will increase their chances of getting their share of the funding pot.

Of course there are also a number of ways in which funders can contribute towards ensuring a more even distribution of resources. It is essential that funding bodies stay informed about pressing social issues affecting both society at large and the local community. This can then lead to regular policy reviews and the implementation of a "proactive" approach where funders actively seek out projects most in need of support. Whilst some funders do focus their support on neglected areas, the vast majority do not, reinforcing an imbalance in the way in which funds are distributed.

In the meantime, however, there is much that "less appealing" organisations can do to make an impact on their own financial state of affairs. This guide aims to show them how...

PART ONE
Recognising the Problem

This section looks at the change in the way in which organisations are being funded. It includes an overview of recent legislation and its effect on statutory funding for the voluntary sector generally. It also looks more specifically at the way in which "non-mainstream" organisations might be affected and at the impact of the funding situation on those awarding contracts, grants or donations to voluntary organisations.

Ways of analysing the problems facing your particular organisation are also outlined with suggested methods of evaluating the work you do. Recognising the problems facing you can lead to positive action to future success.

Case studies in this section are on the Brecon and District Disabled Club and the Life Anew Trust.

1 Introduction

Many people in the voluntary sector feel a great sense of revulsion at the mention of anything to do with "promoting your organisation" and "raising money". One cannot help but feel that there are some very nasty elements attached to the ideas, like "selling out", "buying into the establishment" or "behaving like business". But whatever our discomfort, promoting your organisation (call it "raising your profile" if you prefer) and fundraising are activities that small organisations cannot afford to neglect. Those organisations that promote themselves effectively and invest in fundraising are more likely to survive than those that don't. The current funding climate makes this all the more important.

Raising money and enhancing people's awareness of a particular cause are never easy. All too often, insufficient time and effort are put into this aspect of an organisation's work, perhaps as a result of a poor understanding of the way in which fundraising actually works and the benefits that profile-raising can bring. Nobody parts easily with money, least of all during times of financial difficulty, so it is important that organisations learn how to make their voice heard.

Before they can do this, however, it might be useful to get a brief insight into the problems facing all kinds of small "hard-to-sell" groups as well as those facing funding bodies. Organisations will also need to focus on the specifics of their own organisation before they can move forward.

2 The changing funding scene

One of the factors impacting on funding in England, Wales and Scotland has been the implementation of the NHS and Community Care Act 1990 and to a lesser extent the Local Government Act 1988. These pieces of legislation have resulted in a shift of boundaries between statutory, voluntary and private provision, often with mainstream services receiving the bulk of contract funding and supplementary services being assigned to the bottom of the funding pile. The NHS and Community Care Act by itself provided the legislation necessary for the creation of independent, self-governing NHS trusts. The new NHS market means that NHS trusts now lead the way in charitable fundraising and compete fiercely with charities and other voluntary organisations for funds.

Similarly, the 1988 Education Reform Act in England and Wales has established opted-out schools as charities, adding yet another sector to the scramble for the funding pot.

In Northern Ireland, similar changes are occurring via the Government White Papers "Working for Patients, 1989", "Promoting Better Health, 1987" and "People First: Community Care in Northern Ireland for the 1990s". As a result, Units of Management are being set up to reorganise and improve the planning of health and social care provision. This means that the four health and social services boards for Northern Ireland will no longer provide services directly, but will purchase services from the Units of Management and other agencies via contractual agreements. Although voluntary organisations in Northern Ireland traditionally have had a strong input into government programmes, it is clear that some organisations will find the contract arrangements difficult, particularly where they are competing with hospitals and schools for funding.

Central government funding to voluntary organisations in England, Wales, Scotland and Northern Ireland as a whole increased by around 14% in 1991/92 – a total of £3,387,209,000 was given that year, compared with £2,680,050,000 for 1990/91. Not all of this represents direct grants – much of the funding covers contracts and fees. Central government in England and Wales is also making moves away from their traditional role of providing core funding, increasing pressure on organisations to "diversify their income strategy". Dave Simmonds, Head of Economic and Social Policy at NCVO claims, "There is a shift to wean the voluntary sector off what some ministers call "dependency" on central government funding".

Over the last few years up to 1990/91, other voluntary sector income appears to have been decreasing. For the same period, however, the top 400 fundraising charities saw a substantial increase in their income. Simmonds states, "It is easier for larger organisations to maintain their income. Things are tougher for smaller organisations."*

So what does all this mean? It means that funding for core costs and projects is harder to come by – there is greater competition for available funds created by an increase in need for services (particularly where the state is no longer providing them). There are also changes in the way in which organisations are being funded by local authorities and health authorities. Organisations must ensure that they are fully conversant with these changes, and that they understand the implications for their fundraising.

Whilst all this might mean more money for some organisations, it also means that lesser known smaller organisations which do not provide purchasable services and those which are unable to diversify their services in order to attract contracts, will find raising money very tough.

What kinds of groups are affected and how?

Which groups are we in fact talking about? We're talking about small organisations, specifically those organisations that are a bit different from the traditional children's charity or wildlife fund. These may include charities which have had a history of statutory support, but which are increasingly having to supplement these funds by broadening the scope of their fundraising. It will include non-charitable organisations forced to step up their public fundraising with little practical experience of how to do it, with no existing base to build on and not enough time in which to do it. It will include those causes which are not immediately attractive and where pains have to be taken to explain the importance of the cause, to persuade people to back it. There are many different situations where fundraising will be difficult. It is important to be aware of your particular situation so you can do something to improve your chances. Below is a summary of some of the things that certain kinds of groups may come up against.

---

* The National Lottery, which is being set up by central government will prove a unique opportunity for the voluntary sector and will undoubtedly be the largest general fund for voluntary organisations in the UK. The White Paper concerning the National Lottery confirms that funds distributed from the lottery will be additional money and will not replace grants through other government programmes. It is too early to estimate to what extent small, local "difficult" causes will benefit from lottery funds, although the voluntary sector is lobbying to try to ensure that such organisations are not excluded.

Local projects

As a general rule, local projects find raising money more difficult than large national charities. They have less experience of fundraising and may not have the resources to undertake this work. There are far fewer funders to whom they can appeal and they may therefore have become dependent on local government funding. Some areas of the country are worse off than others. Most trust resources are administered and distributed in the South East; Liverpool and Newcastle both have a lively trust sector; Manchester and Sheffield do not.

Organisations active in Scotland, Northern Ireland or Wales also fare badly. For example, a paper looking at trust funding for the voluntary sector in Scotland, produced by the Scottish Council for Voluntary Organisations, estimated that on average only 5% of the expenditure of grant-making trusts goes to organisations based in Scotland.

Groups in rural areas

Rural groups, particularly in England, experience difficulty because our society is so urban-biased, with London being perceived as the centre of activity. Funders make no distinction between projects based in towns or cities and those based in the country – all projects are measured with an urban yardstick.

Factors relating specifically to rural groups are not often taken into consideration when grants policies are drawn up or when assessing applications. The costs of running services in a rural area are nearly always higher than the costs of running the same services in an urban area. Sparsity in population means that transport services or mobile offices may need to be set up. A group will take longer to set up a project in a rural area than in an urban area owing to the distances that need to be travelled to get to committee meetings, visit people, build the organisation's credibility, develop contacts, etc. Charities in rural areas are more likely to provide a range of general services, rather than just cater for one particular client group, again because of sparse populations.

If these points are not taken on board, it may mean that a funder does not fund a rural project because it seems too expensive, its services seem too diverse and do not appear to have enough users and it looks as though the project will take too long to set up.

Alongside this, earmarked funds from the Rural Development Commission are generally awarded to groups within the designated Rural Development Areas and Rural Coalfield Areas and must be matched by support from elsewhere. Other government funds earmarked for rural groups make the bizarre assumption that every rural group is an environmental or conservation project! Carol Young, Head of the Rural Team at the National Council for Voluntary Organisations says: "There is no earmarked pot of money that a rural group in England can feel good about approaching."

On top of all this, rural groups often find themselves in areas where Councils for Voluntary Service are either non-existent or only very poorly resourced. The result is that rural groups frequently do not have the kind of access to information and advice that groups in urban areas take for granted.

Groups campaigning for political change

Another kind of group which is likely to experience difficulties in raising money is the political campaigning organisation. It is generally accepted by the Charity Commission that most charities can undertake some form of campaigning, as long as it is not a primary purpose of the organisation and is ancillary to the main work. Party political advocacy is always prohibited. There are some organisations whose activities are too political for them to able to obtain charitable status. The majority of funders specifically require organisations they intend to support to have charitable status and even where this is not the case, most are only able to fund work of a charitable nature.

Campaigning organisations are also unlikely to get statutory funding, even though they are not necessarily exempt from it. This is either because their campaigning will "bite the hand that feeds them" or because offering such support will cause too much controversy. Even if statutory funding is a possibility, many groups would be reluctant to accept it anyway because it could mean having to compromise principles. This leaves campaigning organisations generally with little other choice than to rely on membership subscriptions, donations from affiliated organisations (e.g. political parties sympathetic to the cause), legacies and fundraising events.

Additionally, a campaigning organisation may not have the same key opportunities to raise its profile as, for example, a charity providing a tangible service (e.g. where case studies of individuals can form part of an organisation's argument). An organisation campaigning for nuclear disarmament or an environmental group, for example, often has to relate its publicity to a media news story, (e.g. a nuclear accident or an oil spill). As Anna-Zohra Tikly, CND's fundraiser states, "Campaigning groups are dependent on how they are perceived by the media. Our media image directly affects the kind of fundraising we can do."

Another disadvantage faced by campaigning groups is the lack of information and advice specifically aimed at these groups. Many advice agencies assume they are dealing with organisations with charitable status and fail to acknowledge the obvious differences and difficulties of fundraising when an organisation is not politically neutral.

Organisations whose cause is "controversial"

If you are a group dealing with what some people consider a "controversial" issue, you are also in for a raw deal. A so-called "controversial" cause might include a Black-led initiative, a refugee organisation, a charity for people with mental illnesses, a lesbian or gay group, an organisation run by and for disabled people – in fact any issue or area of which people are ignorant or where there is prejudice.

Often, the statutory sector has been the only source of funding such organisations have been able to obtain. But with the contract culture permeating local government, cut-backs in funding mean that even these avenues of support are becoming less of an option. With only a few trusts specifying a grant-making policy positively favouring groups that are perceived as "unpopular", the steady erosion of statutory funding means that many of these groups will come unstuck.

Whilst it is true to say that today's "controversial" or "unpopular" cause may well be tomorrow's "trendy" cause (as has been the case with homelessness and HIV/AIDS), it is also true to say that a change in public attitudes towards a particular issue rarely benefits the smaller organisation dealing with that issue – on the whole, it is the large national organisations that stand to gain from such a turnaround. Additionally, smaller organisations dealing with certain issues frequently fail to perceive themselves as part of the voluntary sector, which means they have limited access to resources and information, often resulting in a lack of expertise in traditional charity fundraising.

Of course there are organisations which fall into more than one of the above categories. For example, yours may be a local project run by/ for black disabled people in Scotland. In such a case, you are likely to face more than just one level of discrimination and even greater difficulty in getting the resources you need to operate effectively.

How are funders and donors affected?

If small "non-mainstream" charities are affected by the changes in the way funds are being allocated, what about the funders or donors themselves? The new funding scene has created a greater competitiveness between voluntary organisations and a need for these organisations to broaden their base of support. Funders will have to cope with an increase in the number of appeals and this will inevitably result in more stringent rules about who will be funded. Different funders will prioritise their funding according to their own aims and objectives.

Statutory authorities

Statutory authorities, which need to fulfil their responsibilities to the community by purchasing services, are increasingly funding services through contracts as a way of pursuing their own agenda and cutting costs. Gone are the days when local government was able to award grants for progressive, innovative projects, outside their mainstream programmes.

Statutory authorities now have very limited budgets and will look for cheaper ways of providing "essential" services, for which they are responsible and which they themselves used to provide. The local council or health authority will look to contract organisations which have a track record of providing these services, and which can do so at a competitive rate. Inevitably, if you are a project providing a service which is innovative and forward thinking but which is perceived as supplementary rather than as essential, a statutory funder may applaud you but is unlikely to support you.

Grant-making trusts

Because grant-making trusts are set up specifically to give grants, they are in a position to respond positively to appeals from "unpopular" causes or from projects in remote parts of the country. They have a special role in promoting innovation and in helping those organisations who find it most difficult to help themselves. Yet those organisations that are attractive to the public are also often attractive to trusts. Although there are a number of trusts which are progressive and which actively seek out projects that are neglected by other funders, many trusts are quite conservative in their grant-giving. Popular areas of support include medical research and large building appeals. Because all grant-making trusts are deluged with applications for funding, the main focus of the majority of grant-making trusts will be on projects which can offer value for money (for example, by demonstrating that an idea has the potential to be used as a model for duplication elsewhere).

However, there is some good news. New and quite substantial sources of charitable funds have emerged in recent years. For example, Charity Projects was established in 1984 to fund grass roots voluntary organisations in the UK, working, for example, in the areas of alcohol and drug dependency, homelessness and disability. BBC Children in Need also focuses much of its giving on small locally-based projects. Additionally, Business in the Community and The Prince's Trust were instrumental in establishing Black economic development projects following inner city unrest in the mid-1980s.

Companies

Companies make donations for a range of reasons, many of which are based on what is in it for them. In difficult economic times, this aspect is even more important. It is hard to give large sums of money away if employees are subject to a wage freeze or redundancies, or if profits (and shareholder dividends) have dropped. A company may want to concentrate its support on local projects in areas where it has a plant or factory in order to ensure good relations with the local community or will support projects in which employees are involved, sometimes through matching funds raised by staff – this reinforces good staff relations.

Another aspect of a company's donations to the voluntary sector is self-promotion. Companies frequently fund a voluntary organisation via their marketing or promotions budget rather than their charitable donations budget, and will expect to gain substantial publicity from the sponsorship expenditure. This will only work with "safe" organisations. An "unpopular" cause has little to offer a company on this score. However, the cause may relate in some way to the company's activities, e.g. a drugs manufacturer may consider funding a health project to promote its public image (although the health project may be reluctant to accept such a donation).

Whilst self-promotion is an important factor in the way in which corporate donations are made, it is not unheard of for companies simply to give donations because they believe a particular project is a good idea. Often these are for traditional causes, such as scout clubs or children's welfare. There are companies whose outlook is relatively progressive, but these are very few and the amounts they have to give away are quite small. Again, because companies will be deluged with appeals, it is likely that they will focus on organisations that they know about and that have a good track record.

Individuals

Donations from individuals are a great fundraising opportunity for voluntary organisations. Support can be given through a subscription to an organisation's newsletter, membership, participation in a fundraising event, street or door-to-door collections (see *Raising money and getting support from individuals*, page 79) or many of the other fundraising ideas that charities have developed. Those individuals who already support your organisation through subscriptions will do so because they or their relatives are service users themselves, or just because they feel good about supporting the organisation. As there are a large number of causes trying to attract donors, it is not unlikely that the people who have supported an organisation because it makes them feel good, will put their allegiance elsewhere, if they are not getting what they expect out of supporting the organisation, or if something else catches their eye.

As people are being bombarded by charitable appeals sent through the post and advertisements in the press, on TV and on hoardings, they will be choosy about whom they support. More often than not, they will support a nationally known organisation, or one that works in the area in which they live. As a general rule, donors want to fund projects with a good reputation, a track record of achievement and which are (or seem to be) cost-effective.

3 All about your organisation

Before a charity can embark on any kind of programme or strategy to enhance its fundraising potential, it is important to look at the overall operations of the organisation. You will want to know where you are in the scheme of things and where you hope to be. This means you will have to define your current situation clearly by looking at your aims, values, objectives and your strategy. You can then review your situation and develop a way forward.

Where you're at

Every organisation should have a statement of its aims, values, objectives and an outline of a strategy. These are important in that they underpin your everyday work. To gain a clear picture of "where you're at", you will find it helpful to look at these aspects of your organisation. They can mark your progress to date and highlight where improvements can be made.

Aims

The aims of an organisation provide the focal point for all the work that it undertakes. Make sure that you come to a general consensus about your main goal. Your aim is likely to be quite broad, for example, "to promote the welfare of older people".

Values

The values of any organisation provide a basis for all decision-making. Your values might relate to a wide range of areas – from service provision to internal staff relations. For example, one of the organisation's main statements of values might relate to its commitment to equal opportunities both in service provision and in its dealings with staff and volunteers. It could also focus on a commitment to providing low-cost, high quality services. You will need to decide how you are going to get your values across to your supporters and service users.

Objectives

Your objectives can be outlined in what some people call a "mission statement". Your objectives will describe the work you do to achieve your aims. For example, your objectives might be "to provide home care for older people".

Strategy

A strategy points the way forward to meeting the aims and objectives of your organisation. It might include raising £x to pay y number of new carers for the service. Your strategy will be a plan which can facilitate meeting your objectives. You will need to look at your strategy and ask whether it measures up to this task. Is it a long-term strategy? Does it provide your organisation with direction? How regularly is it reviewed? Why is it the right strategy for you now? It is vital that you review your strategy on a regular basis – this will enable you to monitor your progress and to look at areas which need improvement.

What's the problem?

It is important to have a clear view of your organisation and the way it functions, including aspects of the organisation that hold it back. This can then enable you to think about ways of counteracting these problems and reinforcing the positive aspects of your project.

Doing research and evaluating your work

To find out how well you are doing and how other people perceive you, you will have to conduct some basic research. You can do this by putting together a simple questionnaire and mailing this to your supporters, service users, funders, etc.

Make sure that you explain to people why you are carrying out the survey and give people the option of completing the questionnaire anonymously. The kinds of questions you ask will depend on your particular organisation and the services you provide but you might need to know something about the person who is filling in the questionnaire. You could ask a few basic personal questions, such as age, gender, racial origin, etc., and whether the person answering the questionnaire is a member of the organisation or how often he or she uses your services. This sort of personal information can be useful in identifying your current supporters and service users, and can help you to direct your future publicity to encourage support from communities which might be under-represented.

You can then move on to information relating specifically to your organisation. Questions like "How well has the organisation met your needs?" "How do you feel about the way the organisation operates?" "How well do you rate the organisation's publicity material?" might be useful. It is often better not to leave questions open-ended – let people tick a box with the appropriate answer. For example:

How do you rate the organisation's publicity material?
fabulous ☐   O.K. ☐   a total waste of space ☐

This will make it easier for people to fill in the questionnaire and easier for you to evaluate. Always give people extra space so that they can comment freely as well. Remember to thank people at the bottom of the questionnaire for giving their time to fill it in and don't forget to include a stamped addressed envelope so that it is easy for people to return.

If you want to reach out beyond your existing support base, you could try to get the questionnaire included in another organisation's magazine or newsletter. Or you may need to do some market research through interviews, surveys or externally facilitated discussion groups. Here you might want to take professional advice. A local market research agency might be persuaded to donate its time free, or a local university marketing course might be looking for projects for its students (if this is the case, it is always worth getting in touch with the Tutor first, to ensure adequate briefing is given).

The responses you receive will give you some idea of the areas in which your organisation is successful and those in which there is room for improvement. For example, if the majority of respondents say that you react slowly to enquiries, you will need to ensure a speedier reaction. This might mean getting more volunteers involved. Or it might be that people believe that you do not run efficiently. In this case you will need to demonstrate that you *are* efficient by undertaking a review of the way in which things are done. You may discover that your organisation could operate more effectively and efficiently if, for example, work schedules are planned differently, or if more volunteers, or more paid staff are brought in. It might even mean having an external audit or evaluation taken by an independent organisation.

Indeed, questionnaires and surveys can form part of your organisation's evaluation process. Evaluations are an effective way of making sure that your organisation operates in a way which best meets its objectives. They are important because they provide an external objective assessment of the quality of your work and can be used to support the claim that you are a successful effective organisation. They can also help you to identify ways of improving, and therefore put you over as an organisation committed to quality and success.

Remember to try to evaluate not just what you do (your output), but the impact of what you do (the outcome). Deciding what are relevant outcomes for your work is part of setting your objectives. For example, if you are running a hostel for homeless people, getting them into permanent accommodation or into a settled way of life might be the desired outcome.

Addressing the need

All too often people get bogged down by everyday routine only to lose sight of the overall picture. They may fail to recognise changing needs as they occur. Keeping informed about your particular issue will help you to assess your services and how effective they are. Has the need that your organisation is meeting increased or decreased in recent times? Are there more or fewer agencies dealing with the need? What are the current trends? Where does your organisation fit in? These aspects can also be measured by undertaking surveys, e.g. you could get a rough idea of local government's response to the need by sending out questionnaires (see *Doing research and evaluating your work*, page 20).

It is also useful to look at the ways in which you try to meet the need. Should your organisation approach the problem differently? Or can you justify the approach you are taking? You will need to look at whether you are running your services cost-effectively. Does your particular approach require extra resources? Are you happy about the quality and quantity of your work at its present cost? All these aspects of your work need careful consideration and will influence the way you develop your strategy.

Analysing the problem

To further clarify the position of your organisation it is often helpful to undertake what is known as a "**SWOT** Analysis". Pretentious as this may sound, it is actually quite a handy way of remembering to look at your **Strengths** and **Weaknesses**, at the **Opportunities** and impending **Threats** facing you in your work. This kind of "analysis" can also contribute towards your revised strategy and can give you a detailed breakdown of what you have to offer and of where you can tackle specific problems.

Your strengths might be:
◆ the quality of your work
◆ the commitment of your staff and volunteers
◆ your volunteer input
◆ community support
◆ user involvement
◆ your track record
◆ your effectiveness and value for money
◆ your membership
◆ your goals and values
◆ the beneficial impact of your services on those who use them

You will need to find ways of providing evidence of your strengths in order to be able to use these points when you present your case, e.g. using statistics and case studies (see *Presenting your case*, page 31).

Your weaknesses could be:
◆ other people's perceptions of your organisation and its work
   e.g. they don't understand, other causes are more important, they
   think it isn't important, they don't like the way you work, etc.

- your style and method of working
  e.g. you're too political, you don't have time for fundraising, PR, development, you don't have any famous trustees or patrons, etc.
- your approach to fundraising
  e.g. you don't know how to ask, there's nobody to ask, you don't like doing fundraising, you've been given an unrealistic target with an inadequate budget, it failed last time, the committee doesn't care, you're slowly going bust, everyone's depressed, etc.

You will need to find a way of overcoming each of your weaknesses. For example, if someone's perception of your organisation is a problem, you will have to take that on board and find ways of challenging that perception (see *Challenging stereotypes*, page 30). Or if you don't know how to ask for funding, it might be an idea to go on a fundraising course. In addition, you should focus on possible opportunities and impending threats.

Your opportunities could be:

- new charitable money is available specifically for your kind of work
- the National Lottery
- you have recently made some personal contacts which could lead to support
- you have discovered a new local funder that nobody else has heard about

Look out for information about new initiatives and developments by keeping informed. Make sure that you make the most of every opportunity as it presents itself to you.

The threats to your organisation might be:-

- there are too many organisations chasing after not enough money
- the criteria of funding programmes have moved away from your own priorities
- major funders are strapped for cash and are likely to cut back on their support
- the contract culture is shifting the emphasis away from grants to contracts

If you can recognise the threats as they come up, you can do something to safeguard your situation. In some cases, you might be able to turn a threat into an opportunity, e.g. the fact that the emphasis of a funding programme is changing may seem like a threat, but if you can find ways of adapting a particular project to meet the new criteria, this threat could become an opportunity.

CASE STUDY

Brecon and District Disabled Club

This organisation, which was set up in 1985, provides a transport service for elderly and disabled people of all ages in the Brecon and Crickhowell areas of rural Wales. It has one main office and a small sub office in Crickhowell. The club has eight paid employees and 104 volunteers and an annual income of around £70,000 which it raises from local government and charitable trusts.

The charity has established a good track record and its dial-a-ride service is tangible evidence of its work, highlighting the charity's profile amongst the general public and funders. Indeed, the charity received a joint grant of £19,000 from the local county council and borough council as well as one contract from the local education authority to provide transport for children with learning difficulties. Dial-a-Ride has been able to sell its services on the basis of its unique provision of wheelchair clamping and has set up a trading company in preparation for further contracts with the local authority.

The charity has also approached grant-making trusts for funding. Says John Price, General Manager, "Our success with charitable trusts is due to the commitment and skill of the volunteers who give up their weekends to make applications. We also have a tailor-made computer programme, funded by the Charities Aid Foundation, that gives very detailed information on about 2,800 trusts." Whilst only very few companies have been responsive to the charity's appeals for support, the charity has managed to gain corporate support at a local level. "We've had no joy from large national companies, but we have had sponsorship from a few local companies", claims Price.

The charity has no marketing staff but it has nevertheless developed a profile amongst local funding bodies not least by focusing on aspects of its service that make it unique and by looking imaginatively at ways of funding services in the future.

CASE STUDY

The Life Anew Trust

The Life Anew Trust was set up in 1982 to provide residential care for people with chronic alcohol or drug dependency. People who are dependent on drugs and alcohol are not commonly viewed with great sympathy by either the public or funding institutions. The problem is perceived as being "self-inflicted" and so not as deserving as other forms of illness.

In the three years leading up to 1 April 1993, the Life Anew Trust had managed to keep its head above water, with income coming from diverse sources – principally fees for the core residential treatment, the family programme and external training work supplemented by grants from health authorities and donations from trusts, companies and individuals. Thirty per cent of the charity's income came from centrally funded income support payments which only contributed to social care costs. Treatment had to be heavily subsidised from other funds. Over the last two years a growing number of patients have been funded as Extra Contractual Referrals by health authorities.

However, the introduction of Community Care on 1 April 1993 posed considerable financial and administrative problems for the trust. Principal responsibility for purchasing appropriate care for alcohol or drug users now falls to local authorities using money transferred from the Department of Social Security. Because the government reneged on a promise to ring-fence money for the social care of alcohol and drug dependent people, residential services must now compete alongside services for elderly people, disabled people and people with learning difficulties. The level of social services contribution has to be negotiated with each individual authority and the trust deals with over 40, many of whom have insufficient funds even to cover social care.

The consequent lack of income, partly caused by awkward assessment procedures, means the trust has had to cut costs drastically and find alternative ways of attracting income. It has developed training services for GPs and other healthcare professionals as well as education and training for the workplace and health promotion for schools. One result is that British Rail have been referring employees who need treatment and buying in training packages on an area basis. A major national charity is also negotiating a training package. The trust hopes that as its reputation spreads, further arrangements of this kind will be made particularly with local employers.

Additionally, a fundraising appeal for a "fighting fund" of £200,000, which together with cost cutting, is estimated to be enough money to "get us through the cash famine that we are going to encounter until the local authorities have sorted out their various responsibilities", according to Wallis Hunt, the trust's Fundraiser. So far £70,000 has been raised thanks largely to the generosity of former patients and to good relations with grant-making trusts and individuals who have provided support in the past. One foundation has volunteered a £60,000 interest-free loan when Life Anew's fighting fund reaches £140,000.

The Life Anew Trust has so far survived the funding crisis by its readiness and ability to enter into formal contractual relationships with statutory authorities and a flexible and forward-thinking approach. The trust is determined that no potential source will be left untapped.

PART TWO
Promotion and PR

This section suggests ways of presenting your case effectively, to persuade the public that your cause is worth supporting. This includes ideas on how to challenge stereotypes that are commonly attributed to the users of your service or to the kind of work that you do and how to demonstrate that you are meeting a need.

It also looks at promoting both your cause and your organisation through direct contact with the public, such as giving talks, organising open days, etc. and indirectly through, for example, mailings, posters, etc. There is also information on promoting your cause and organisation to the media, including writing a news release, approaching different kinds of media and media planning.

The section then moves on to look at ways of reinforcing your organisation's credibility by focusing on your name and reputation and on your image and how you relate to the public and to your supporters.

Articles in this section are on "Images: Cause or Effect?" by Sharon Welch, Save the Children Fund, which explores ways of promoting your cause without reinforcing negative images, and "Setting up a PR system" by Becky Glenister, Charityfair, which shows how easy it is to put a PR system into operation.

Case studies are on Gemma, the Gender Dysphoria Trust International and the Legalise Cannabis Campaign.

1 Introduction

How the public sees your cause is important. The reason for this is simple – people have to be convinced that the cause is worthy and worthwhile supporting. If someone is unaware of the importance of the issue or areas you are working in, they will probably not be interested in supporting your organisation. Their interest will be caught by what they believe to be more pressing causes.

As well as helping to raise awareness, you will be enhancing your organisation's image and convincing people that you are an organisation that should be supported. For example, an organisation like Shelter has managed successfully to raise its profile by putting a great deal of effort into the campaign against homelessness for which there is now much public support. Raising awareness of your cause locally through local campaigning and publicity can also be an effective way of fostering good links with the community in which you operate, and can often result in support both through donations as well as through volunteer involvement.

Raising awareness of your cause isn't something you do once and then assume that it will stay in people's minds; it is something that needs your continuous attention. You will need to make sure that the issue you are dealing with remains in the public eye – otherwise people's awareness will eventually peter out and everyone will carry on thinking that babies and wildlife are the bees knees. Highlighting your cause might even be something that is part of your everyday work so be aware that what you do in this area will contribute towards people's awareness and might mean they will want to give you their undying support.

One of the first things that you might need to do is to put people right about the issue you are working on or about the people who use your services.

2 Making a better case

Persuasion is a central part of promoting your organisation. You will need to put forward a convincing argument in favour of your organisation and the work you do. This might mean you will have to look at dealing with stereotyping as well as at ways of presenting your case effectively.

Challenging stereotypes

Many groups will find that their cause fails to win support because the public has a stereotyped view of the people for whom the group was set up or the work the group was set up to do. Some stereotypes may be harder to break down than others, for example, it is probably going to be easier to educate people about the issues around providing a service in a rural area, than about issues facing people who are gay, because attitudes towards sex and sexuality are far more ingrained than attitudes towards rural issues. People who have a negative view of those who use your services or of the kind of work that you do rarely base their views on objective fact. Their attitudes, which are reinforced by a predominance of negative images in society, are generally emotive and come from fear of the unknown.

The best way to challenge these stereotypes is to identify the kind of views that the public have of the people that use your services or of the work that you do. Often, these views are focused on specific groups who are perceived as:

- the politically subversive – "they're a bunch of lefties"
- the non-conforming – "they're not like us".
- the undeserving – "they should get their act together"

Once you know what you are dealing with, that is, what misconceptions people have when they think about your work or about users of your service, it is up to you then to address these views. Challenging predominant public perceptions can be done by avoiding stereotyped portrayals both in written and visual material and depicting situations which actively confront these stereotypes. This can be achieved both through a factual approach, e.g. using statistics, case histories, other pieces of factual evidence and through visual impact (see *Images: Cause or Effect?*, page 33), such as photographs in your publicity material, posters, etc.

KEY POINTS

- Find out what the stereotype is

- Use images and language that don't conform to the stereotype

- Make positive use of case histories to challenge preconceptions

Release, the national drugs and legal advice agency, operates a 24-hour telephone service to drug users, their families and friends and provides training, publications and education, mainly for professionals working with drug users.

There are a number of stereotypes that people using illicit drugs may be subjected to. These include:

- drug users are automatically heavily into crime
- drug use will lead on to more serious crime
- drug users look scrawny and down at heel
- drug users are from working class backgrounds
- people who get arrested for drug use are Black
- drug users are automatically bad parents

Release aims to counteract these perceptions in all the work that it undertakes. One specific way of doing this is to avoid using language which sounds judgemental, such as addict, pusher, etc. and replacing it with an appropriate, more neutral alternative, e.g. drug user, drug supplier.

Release training challenges stereotyping by using scenarios for case studies that do not conform to the typical public misconceptions already outlined. For example:

"Harriet is a thirty-two year-old heroin user. She has been using heroin for the last six years. Having been arrested and charged with possession of a class A drug, her main concern now is that her employers should not find out. She is a personnel officer in a large company. How would you advise her?"

Additionally, any photographs used by Release, such as in annual reports, do not conform to stereotypes. For example, the organisation is currently looking at its publicity, and posters depicting a police arrest will avoid showing a Black person being arrested. Likewise, other examples used will demonstrate that drug use is something that affects everyone.

Presenting your case

As well as actively turning stereotypes on their head, you will need a statement in all your publicity or in your applications to funders about why the work that is being done is valuable and worthy of support. In order to do this you will have to demonstrate that there is a need for the services your organisation is providing. This involves:

◆ describing the problem, e.g. "there are x number of ex-offenders without jobs." Back up what you say with concrete evidence, either through statistics, case studies or other factual evidence.

◆ saying what it is that your organisation is doing to tackle the problem, e.g. "we provide training and advice for unemployed ex-offenders." Describe the services you provide and how many people use them.

31

KEY POINTS

☞ Demonstrate that there is a problem

☞ Show how you are solving that problem

☞ Make your cause relevant to the person in the street

- showing how your service has contributed towards solving the problem – "x% of the people using our service have now got jobs." Think about the outcomes of what you are doing, rather than simply describe what you do. Reinforce your case by using statistics.

- showing the solutions by illustration with case study examples. If for reasons of confidentiality, this is not possible, you can always create a composite based on fact, e.g. "James is a 55 year-old ex-offender who, after attending one of our training courses, now works as an administrator at a marketing company."

In the examples you choose and the arguments you use to persuade people that your cause is worthy, it is always a good idea to show the woman in the street how the cause is relevant to her. For example, you could demonstrate the benefits of your work to society as a whole by saying how your training programmes for ex-offenders prevent them from re-offending and therefore from posing a threat to society. Show how your work fits in to a wider social context and how it is therefore relevant to everyone and in particular, to the people whose support you are soliciting.

This information can form a framework on which you can then elaborate with information about the history of your organisation and any other information you might want to get across about your cause.

Remember also that if you can demonstrate a high level of profes-sionalism and efficiency in your contact with the public or with funders, this can often help to offset any negative attitudes they may have towards your cause. Your very concern, commitment and energy will help persuade them of the importance of the cause (see *Presenting yourself: image and impression*, page 59).

✍ Images: Cause or Effect?

Sharon Welch, Head of Public Affairs, Save the Children Fund

When small, hard-to-sell groups have a difficult enough time raising funds, is a politically correct approach to getting the message across the right one? What price a no holds barred strategy for promoting projects for ex-offenders or for people with disabilities or with HIV? When the client comes first, what effect does image have on a cause?

The nationally broadcast Telethon which benefited many small causes has now been dropped. The reason given was compassion fatigue. Yet, the main reason for tiredness, particularly among disability groups, was the pitying images and banal treatment of their issue. Or, rather not *their* issue but an issue that should be the concern of everyone.

In this regard, third world charities too have found food for thought. Their stereotyped beneficiaries have not had quite the same "right to reply" as people with disabilities. Yet Western public perception is fed by famine images on television, in newspapers and on radio and often these images are supplied by charities. Eighty-four per cent of people's knowledge and opinions of the developing world come from media and fundraising organisations.

The findings of recent research asked students and tutors what were the numbers of visibly malnourished starving children in the world, the percentage estimated was usually 50 to 75. The real figure is one to two per cent. Similarly, the answer usually given to the question, "how many families in the world are living in absolute poverty?" – is 75 per cent. The real answer is 20-25 per cent. It seems that whatever the questions about the poor in the world, the answers that come back are overwhelmingly negative.

In Britain these ill-informed views contribute to prejudiced ideas and negative opinions of not just the third world but anyone considered to be from the third world. This can work against small – and large – organisations trying to raise funds (in what may seem an unrelated context) for anyone deemed a minority or for anyone with "minority" tastes or needs.

Images have the power to raise money or to raise anxiety – to do good or to do harm. As such images are everybody's business and if the charity business is not to be guilty of complicity, that message is well worth getting across.

Voluntary organisations have been exercised by these issues on and off over the years. Whether the context is an overseas or domestic agenda, the debate about image promotion and their cause or effect requires a lot of unpacking. Small organisations – and indeed some large ones – do not have the time or resources to do justice to the issue. But it can't be ignored either. Finding a way through the debate that leads to practical action is difficult but not impossible.

The main prompts are organisational values, characteristics and philosophy. These should be the basis on which the image of any organisation, commercial or voluntary, should be built. What an organisation does and how it does it should underpin the way it presents itself. This has to be recognised as a basic principle. If not, there is likely to be a dissonance between the reality and the message. A dissonance of words and pictures which undermines organisational objectives and ends up selling people short.

Trustee or management group backing is a powerful statement of the seriousness with which an organisation treats this issue. Organisationally, the way images are presented cannot be dealt with in a vacuum. It is a reflection of the wider good practice of an organisation.

The Save the Children Fund approached implementing an equal opportunities policy by setting up three working groups. One dealing with childcare practice and service to users, the second assessing employment practice issues including gender, sexual orientation, race and disability and the third managing public image and presentation. The synergy required in all three areas was recognised, addressed and new policies were drawn up. Responsibility for the initiatives, their implementation and yearly maintenance was delegated to directors of the organisation by the trustees.

Organisations then should communicate with integrity while striving to gain a wider understanding of their work. So, how best to do that and what are the pitfalls to avoid?

Is there such a thing as a positive or negative image? The answer to this depends literally on how you look at it. Everyone looks at and interprets things differently. Photographs are taken to record and document people and events. What they present as fact depends very much on the circumstances prevailing at the time of photography. The broader context of those details are usually not shown or written about. The photograph then seems to represent a "truth" that is often not questioned. But this "truth" has a power to influence and distort perceptions.

Plus a view of what constitutes a positive or negative image is influenced by all sorts of baggage and hang-ups, historical and ideological. In the BBC's "Black and White Media Show", the point was made that in viewing still or moving pictures, most people are seeking legitimisation for their opinions and attitudes. They do not "see" material which could counter their views. In other words people see what they want to see and, furthermore, they sometimes claim that "positive" images put a gloss on reality. Therefore, presenting a more positive and dignified visual treatment of poor, Black and/ or disabled people is not necessarily a complete solution.

What has also to be remembered is that any type of picture representing marginalised groups or individuals is a small part of a much bigger arena – the limited representation of such people in news coverage, documentaries or current affairs and social reporting. In the day-to-day illustrations of British society, marginalised groups and individuals hardly get a look in. When they do, they are presented as "exotic", unusual or criminal and qualify only in stereotypical terms. Many charity images of course reinforce this. Perhaps, there is no such thing as a positive image but there is a need to challenge perceptions and to avoid stereotyping and in this regard charities have a duty to perform.

How? Are there ways of using images to educate the public? Every communication or appeal cannot be a lesson in the real facts of life of the people depicted. But they can stretch the public imagination by use of challenging and genuinely creative approaches.

Images are often a combination of text and pictures. And images call for context, balance, truth and accuracy if they are to begin to dent stereotypical views. Communications and appeals are usually strengthened, not weakened, by strong facts which do not trivialise, distort or misrepresent. Pictures must not rob their subjects of dignity or reinforce dependency – the medium should not become more important than the message. Patronising, mawkishly sentimental or demeaning words and phrases should be avoided. Powerful facts creatively put over can evoke concern, stimulate interest and lead to action or donations. Advertising and PR agencies who too often resort to cliches need to work much harder for their money. Getting this across requires an understanding of individual responsibility for impacting how people think.

Those who select and use pictures and words must do so with an eye and an ear to how what they select will be received and perceived. If the considerations above are allowed to influence their choices, those choices are in turn likely to influence and shape the way people react. Presenting people with the unfamiliar can create an element of surprise that works for and not against communications objectives. One example of this is a campaign aimed at raising funds for children called "Skip Lunch, Save a Life"; which used an image of a knife, fork and a plate! The campaign contributed to raising twice the targeted income figure.

The brief for that campaign was informed by guidelines about image and presentation. These put an onus on both the commissioners of communications and the commissioned – photographers, illustrators, writers and ad agencies – to ensure that organisational principles match communications practice. Guidelines (which are not very difficult to draw up) help to make image concerns explicit.

Guidelines also remind that shock tactics, for example, the starving baby image, can often undermine and backfire. Research shows that people are often turned off by such tactics. This perhaps is evidence not only that the public can be "educated" about images but also that values-based, objectives-driven communications enhance rather than diminish creativity. And creativity is one of the keys that opens up successful communications.

Small, hard-to-sell groups aiming to win friends and influence people do need to develop their public profile. Communications which promote creativity and accuracy are the preserve of nobody and within the gift of all and do a small cause a great deal of good.

3 Promoting your cause and your organisation

Once you have decided on the message you are going to promote, you will have to look at how you are going to get this message across.

Who is your audience?

There are a number of different channels through which you can direct your publicity. But the first thing that needs to be looked at is who you are trying to address. Do you need to publicise your cause as part and parcel of a funding application to a grant-making trust? Do you want to make an appeal to the general public? What about people who have supported you in the past? Do you need to remind them that you still exist and that your cause is still worthy of their support?

You will need to make sure that you tailor your material or your message to the appropriate audience. This means finding out how much people you are going to address already know about an issue. For example, students might have different levels of awareness of certain issues than, say, business executives. You could do some basic research by devising a questionnaire or monitoring who your supporters are (see *Doing research and evaluating your work*, page 20). You will also need to use language and a style that is appropriate for the audience you are trying to reach. Whoever you are talking to or leafleting, avoid using jargon at all times, but make sure that you are communicating with them effectively.

Contacting people directly

The more personal the approach the better. If you know about the people you are approaching, you can tailor your approach accordingly. There are a number of ways of approaching people directly.

Using personal contacts

Never underestimate the importance of personal contacts. If your organisation has a trustee "with a name", then make sure you take advantage of this. For example, you could get her to endorse your publicity leaflets or sign letters on behalf of your organisation. You could also make the most of any personal contacts that she may have so that you can "get a foot in the door". Once you have done this, arranging a meeting or an opportunity for a presentation shouldn't be a problem.

KEY POINTS

☗ Know who you are trying to reach

☗ Tailor your message appropriately

You could also build a "fundraising committee" or have patrons who are prepared to put some effort into helping to raise support and promote awareness of the issues you are concerned with. Find out who people in your organisation know or have access to who might have or be persuaded to develop a genuine interest in your work (see *Patrons*, page 58).

None of this is very "equal opps.". It favours those with the right connections, and puts traditional charities at an advantage, but it is a sad fact of life that if you know the right people it is easier for you to make headway. Recognising this fact can help you to use the situation to your own benefit.

Giving talks

A talk or presentation can be an excellent opportunity to introduce people to an issue. It can be a very effective way of recruiting support and commitment, particularly if your organisation operates locally. There are a number of organisations which might usefully be approached in this way, for example, schools, local colleges, youth groups, Round Tables, Lions and Rotary Clubs in your area, village meetings, women's guilds, guide and scout groups.

Other voluntary organisations whose work is linked to your own may also be worth approaching. For example, it could be mutually beneficial for a drug agency to give a talk to people working at an alcohol project, or vice versa, where issues are not dissimilar. This could lead to joint projects and other initiatives. There may be other organisations you can think of, which might find it helpful to hear what you have to say.

Whatever you do, don't choose an organisation or group whose interests are likely to be in conflict with the issue you want to promote. For example, it might be better to steer clear of church groups if you want to talk about abortion rights, as feelings might run too high for you or anyone else to be able to gain anything useful from the exercise. It might be more appropriate to give a talk at a local school (if they let you), college or women's group. It is important that you choose the most appropriate audience and ensure that they are likely to be at least not unsympathetic. It is a waste of your time and theirs if it is very unlikely to reap any rewards.

Here are a few tips for presentation-givers:

◆ avoid using jargon

◆ keep your sentences short and simple

◆ speak informally in an accessible way and try to be at ease and friendly

◆ don't pack your talk with too much statistical information (this can put people off)

KEY POINTS

Personal contacts can:

♟ endorse your publicity

♟ get you a "foot in the door"

♟ contribute to fundraising efforts

♟ promote awareness of your cause

- try to make a visual impact, e.g. by using slides or diagrams (this sometimes helps to simplify things and makes the talk more interesting)

- make sure you sound lively and enthusiastic (if you drone on, you are unlikely to inspire anyone)

- don't go on for too long – a 15-minute talk is probably about right, but use your own judgement

- match your talk to the audience's level of awareness

- you may or may not want to consider dressing appropriately

When you present a talk, don't forget to bring along publicity leaflets and materials and any other information about your organisation so that people can make enquiries afterwards. These could have a tear-off form which people can return to you. It is important that you make sure that your organisation has the capacity to deal with enquiries that may be generated as a result of your presentation. For example, get in more volunteers or get an information pack together ready to send out to any inquirers. If you do not deal quickly and efficiently with subsequent callers, the hard work that went into preparing and giving your talk will have been in vain.

Organising open days

Open days can be a way of not only getting local people involved in your cause, but also of keeping your current supporters and service users interested in what you are doing. It can also give your organisation the chance to show potential supporters tangible evidence of your work and to present your case to them on an informal basis.

Open days can be fairly inexpensive, but like everything else they need careful planning if they are to be successful. You will need to decide what format the event will take. Will it be a drinks party with a short presentation? Or an afternoon exhibition of photos of your current projects? Or will you be giving a brief presentation followed by a slide show? Remember to budget for the cost of refreshments, printing and mailing of invitations and other publicity, leaflets for display as well as staff time.

Contacting people on the phone

Some charities contact people over the phone. They get a list of names and phone numbers from the local electoral register and the phone book. This could be an appropriate method if what you are doing is urgent and where you believe people might be interested.

However, there is a strong public reaction against unsolicited phone calls and this method could prove expensive and make you more

---

KEY POINTS

- ☞ Choose an organisation likely to have a sympathetic audience

- ☞ Bring along publicity leaflets and other information about your organisation

- ☞ Make sure your organisation has the resources to deal with resulting enquiries

---

KEY POINTS

- ☞ Decide on the format of the event

- ☞ Put together a realistic budget

London Lighthouse provides support and residential care for people living with HIV and AIDS, through a range of services including counselling, domiciliary support, convalescent respite and day care.

The organisation arranges regular open mornings, which were originally intended to encourage the local community to give their support. However, it is now a very effective way of keeping the organisation in the public eye, raising awareness and challenging misinformation. The open mornings are advertised in the organisation's mailouts and by word of mouth. Between 50 and 100 people attend and the open mornings often comprise an element in the training for nurses and medical students.

The mornings start at 10 am and end at 1 pm and consist of an introductory lecture and slide presentation outlining the history and philosophy of the project, as well as details of any new developments. There is also an opportunity for participants to work through some of the material presented and to ask questions. Once a month, follow-up workshops are organised.

Many of the costs of the open mornings are "invisible", e.g. staff time and materials are part of the organisation's general budget. These costs are covered by charging fees for attendance.

---

enemies than friends. It is up to you to weigh up the benefits and drawbacks. The phone may be problematic for "cold calls" but it can be a powerful tool for developing good relationships between you and your supporters.

If you feel comfortable about phoning people up then make sure you know in advance what you hope to achieve. For example, do you want to let people know about an event that you are organising, or about a talk that you are giving? Are you undertaking a survey about people's attitudes to your cause or the issue you are concerned about? Or do you just want to thank them for the support they have given? Write down what you are going to say in advance, rehearse your approach so your message comes across immediately and effectively and you don't get lost for words.

Here are some things that might be useful when thinking about making phone calls to individuals to people with whom you have had no contact:

◆ introduce yourself and your organisation

◆ say why you are calling

◆ ask if it is a convenient time for them to have a chat and if it isn't ask if you should call back at a more convenient time

◆ remember that people don't have to talk to you so be polite and don't get agitated if people are rude to you.

KEY POINTS

☛ Decide whether or not you could benefit from making "cold calls"

☛ Make sure there is a purpose for your call

☛ Know in advance what you are going to say

Remember, if someone is asking you awkward questions they are more likely to be interested in what you are saying, than if they simply remain silent. Silence is usually a bad sign – it means a person is waiting for you to finish your spiel so that they can get off the phone quickly.

Contacting people indirectly

An indirect approach can be used to get to a very wide audience. Although this does not have the benefit of the personalised approach, it can help to get your message across on a relatively large scale. There are a variety of ways of addressing people indirectly.

Posters and handbills

Posters and handbills are useful for both a local or national campaign or to publicise a local event. They can easily be put in places like community centres and schools, which will help to attract the support of the local population. In the case of a national awareness-raising campaign, they can be distributed to sympathetic organisations around the country. Here are a few things you might like to take into account when designing posters or handbills.

◆ Make sure your poster or handbill is eye-catching – black and white posters or posters with just one colour other than black are cheaper to produce and can often be more effective than a poster using several colours.

◆ Keep it simple – try not to cram the poster or handbill full with information that isn't relevant, but do make sure that there is a contact name, address and phone number so that people can find out more about your cause and if appropriate a helpline or advice line phone number. If you are organising an event, make sure all the details are given, e.g. date, time, venue, cost, whether there is a creche, disabled access, whether there will be any celebrities. Again a contact name and phone number for enquiries is a must.

◆ Keep your message clear – make sure that your message can be grasped immediately and easily. Trying to be witty or funny may not come off, so it is probably better to be direct and to the point.

◆ Shop around for a reasonably-priced printer and get quotes from more than one. Some printers give non-profit organisations discounts so make sure you ask.

Think carefully about where you put your posters and handbills – strategic positioning can make all the difference. For instance, try to avoid putting a poster next to a bigger more striking poster or alongside many others as it will be competing for attention. Make sure that your poster or handbill is put somewhere where it is likely to be seen by a lot of people.

Leaflets

Every organisation should have at least one leaflet about the kind of work that it does, which can be handed out to people at events or at door-to-door collections or sent in a mailing. These are quite easy to produce and can be relatively inexpensive. You don't need anything glossy – a black and white four-page A5 leaflet is perfectly adequate, but take care that it is clear, well-presented and accessibly written.

It should contain information about the history of your organisation and the work you do. Don't forget to put a contact address and phone number so that people can get further information – or better still a reply coupon, so that the sender can tick areas of interest or ways in which they would like to support you. Make sure that you are able to respond to enquiries effectively. To keep costs down, look around for a reasonably priced printer or one that can give you a special deal – perhaps agreeing to do the printing for free if you pay for the paper (and you can always ask a paper merchant to donate the paper from an end-of-line).

Mailings

Mailings are a good way of reminding previous supporters and members (whose names and addresses you will of course have on record!) of the importance of your work. You can use a letter format to inform people about a particular initiative, fundraising event or to make a general appeal for support, whether financial or through contributing to a campaign. Keep your letter to one or two sides of A4 and be concise and to the point. To make your mailing cost-effective, it may be worth considering putting in a leaflet, an appeal brochure or other material that you have about your organisation.

You can also do "cold" mailings (mailings to people with whom you have had no contact). You should think carefully about doing cold mailings – it is often less effective than approaching people with whom you have had some contact, however tentative.

One way of reaching a wider audience is to tap into other organisation's mailing lists and perhaps doing shared mailings. If you are thinking of swapping mailing lists you will have to consider the impact this could have on your image – supporters and members may be annoyed if they find their names and addresses have been passed on to another organisation. You could also use a mailing house who will send out your material for you. Mailing houses are advertised in the charity press.

It is better to be informative about important developments in the field rather than to make frequent general appeals for support. Constant requests for money just to keep your organisation going have been known to put off people who are already involved in an organisation. However, those who do support you may be very happy to support a new development if you can make a good case.

KEY POINTS

- Make sure you have at least one leaflet describing your work

- Make it clear, well-presented and accessibly written

- Don't forget to put a contact address and phone number or reply coupon

---

KEY POINTS

- Use these to provide supporters with information about new initiatives and events

- Make your mailing cost-effective, by including other information about your organisation

Anti-Slavery International, a small organisation in London campaigning for human rights uses mailings to make appeals for donations and to encourage people to contribute to its lobby against exploitation.

The organisation never undertakes "cold" mailings, as its profile is not high enough for this to meet with much success. Instead, it approaches its 1,800 members and those 4,500 supporters who have made one-off donations. Mailings vary from general appeals (no more than twice a year) and letters trying to persuade supporters to become members, to newsletters and information about how members can contribute to a specific campaign.

The organisation uses a simple approach, word-processing letters carefully and avoiding a glossy look which could convey the impression of wasting resources. Occasionally, the letter may include a black and white photo, if it is relevant. Whilst the return is not as high as a television or radio appeal, the Society has found that it only takes a few large donations to make a significant return. Mailings have also been very useful in keeping members informed about the Society's work and in awareness-raising.

Approaching the media

There are a variety of different media that you can use. It is up to you to decide which is most appropriate, for your particular circumstances. It is important to try to gain the support of the community you are aiming to serve. For example, if you are a local anti-racist action group concerned with the levels of racist attacks in your neighbourhood and you want to get the support of the local community, it would be most effective to publicise your cause in a local newspaper or through poster displays at your community centre.

If you wanted to make people aware of the levels of racist attacks in your area on a much broader scale, your publicity will need to reach a wider audience, so the national press or radio might be more appropriate. It is therefore important that you know who you want to reach.

How do you communicate with the media?

The standard way of communicating with the media – whether it is the press, radio or television – is through a news release. A news release is a brief summary or statement drawing attention to something new, original or enlightening. For instance, you might be approaching the media because you want to make a point concerning the impact of new legislation on the people who use your services; or you might be launching a new initiative; or publishing a research report.

There are a whole range of reasons for wanting to contact the media. The news release is the most appropriate way of doing this, because it provides the media with succinct information in a format which can be easily and quickly adapted to make a story. It can also give you the opportunity to highlight the key features about the case you are making for your organisation.

A news release should begin with a snappy heading which summarises in a few words what the rest of the news release is about. The first paragraph should outline the most important points, and these will reinforce the headline. It should deal with what the problem is, who is responsible for it and how you fit in. Any subsequent paragraphs flesh out the backbone that you have given in the headline and first paragraph.

When you are writing a news release, you should bear in mind that the media will focus on something that *makes news*. For example, let's say you want to publicise the fact that you are setting up a counselling and advice scheme for young homeless people. A headline like "Hope for Bradford's 2,000 homeless young people, as charity launches new advice scheme" is probably more likely to receive a media response than a headline like "Charity sets up scheme for homeless young people". This is because the first headline locates a specific problem and shows how the charity is helping to deal with that problem. It also adds a "newsy" angle. The second headline is too general and quite vague and leaves a lot of questions unanswered.

The first paragraph could read something like "First Base, the first ever scheme of its kind to be set up in Bradford, is being launched by Homes Now, a local charity. First Base, which will be up and running in December, will provide information and advice ranging from health care to getting a job. It will also provide counselling and a hostel referral programme."

The second paragraph could expand on the above information and might even include a quote: "First Base was set up with a grant of £30,000 from the Money for Homes Trust and will form part of a whole range of services for young homeless people organised by Homes Now. Ms Akbar, Director, comments: 'We believe this addition to our services will make a real difference to people's lives, but there is much more that can be done and we will continue to put the case for further government action to provide homes for homeless people.'"

At the bottom of the page you should put the name of the person to be contacted for further information and their phone number. Remember to date the news release. If you are a charity you should quote your registered charity number (as indeed you should on all publicity material you produce).

You might want to embargo the information. To do this you must include a statement saying that the information in the news release cannot be used until a specific time on a specific date. This will be useful if you want to give the media advance information on, say, the text of a speech due to be given by someone, or if there is a news angle

KEY POINTS

- Make sure your heading is short, snappy and summarises the main points of the news release

- Provide a "newsy" angle

- Give a contact name and phone number

to the story (such as a set of statistics). The embargo makes sure that the information is not made public until a specific date. This allows you to control the release of the information (if the information is used) and also assures the editor that a rival will not have already used the news item.

Homes Now's final news release might look something like this:

News Release
20th June 1994

Hope for Bradford's 2,000 homeless young people, as charity launches new advice scheme

First Base, the first ever scheme of its kind to be set up in Bradford, is being launched by Homes Now, a local charity. First Base, which will be up and running in December, will provide information and advice ranging from health care to getting a job. It will also provide counselling and a hostel referral programme.

First Base was set up with a grant of £30,000 from the Money for Homes Trust and will form part of a whole range of services for young homeless people organised by Homes Now. Ms Akbar, Director, comments: 'We believe this addition to our services will make a real difference to people's lives, but there is much more that can be done and we will continue to put the case for further government action to provide homes for homeless people.'

For further information about First Base and about Homes Now, please contact Ms Akbar, Director on (telephone number)

Homes Now is a registered charity no. 9110521

It can be a good idea to follow up your news release with a phone call to the person it was sent to, to check that it arrived safely and to find out whether they require any further information. Whatever you do, resist the temptation of pestering them to carry the story – just try to be as helpful as you can.

Now that you've written your news release, you can start to think about whom to approach. The media is a general term which includes the press, radio and television. Below are a few things to think about first.

Newspapers, magazines and journals

Local and regional newspapers are a very useful way of informing local people about your cause and encouraging volunteer involvement. For example, you can let your newspaper know about an event taking place whether it is a stunt to raise awareness or a fundraising event by sending in your news release. Make sure you approach the appropriate person by first checking the name and job title with the paper. If a reporter at a local or regional paper gives you coverage, be sure to stay in touch with her. Try to build a relationship with her and get her interested in what you are doing. She may help you out in the future and you may be able to help her out by providing a "story".

Getting coverage in the national press is more difficult for a local project or for a very small organisation but it is not impossible. What you need to remember is that the national press will want a *national story*. This means that your event or news will have to do the following:

◆ be of national significance

◆ be of topical interest (for example, if your organisation has recently been affected by the implementation of a particular piece of legislation that has received recent media coverage)

◆ say something that will make an impact

Magazines or specialist journals are very useful vehicles for informing an audience that is likely to be sympathetic to your cause. Be careful with your choice of magazine. For example, if you are an organisation trying to raise awareness of lesbian issues, then your first port of call should be the lesbian and/or gay press. This will ensure that you stay in touch with your own constituency of support.

However, in order to raise the issue with a wider audience, you will need to approach other women's magazines. Avoid those magazines that are likely to have a hostile editorial outlook or readership. They will either not be interested in your story or be looking to report you negatively. Go for some of the less conservative women's magazines (e.g. Every Woman).

Similarly, if you are a Black group or a disability organisation, you could be looking at ways not just of keeping Black people and disabled people informed of the current issues, but also of broadening your scope by approaching magazines and newspapers that do not specifically focus on these groups, but which are likely to address a sympathetic audience. You may want to send a covering letter outlining why a magazine's particular readership should be interested in your organisation's story. The same goes for campaigning organisations, rural groups, in fact any type of organisation.

You will know what is right for your organisation, but you should not simply be seeking to reach the "converted". Try to look to broadening the audience for your message.

There are various ways in which articles can be presented. These are:

The News Story – this is an up-to-date piece of news presented factually and in a detached manner. The structure of the piece usually follows the structure of your news release, i.e. it will have all the important information in the first paragraph, with further paragraphs filling in the details. Many reporters will take the text from your news release verbatim if it is well-written. You should contact the News Editor or the appropriate correspondent(s), e.g. if you are an HIV/AIDS charity, with information about a new piece of research on the spread of HIV, it would be useful to get in touch with both the Health and the Social Services correspondents by name.

Features – these are usually longer articles of a topical nature with room for comment and personal opinion. They may involve various points of view. The article may be about something that is already in the public eye and so might contribute to public debate. It may be something new which the editor would like to bring to public attention. Or it might just be a good story of interest to the readers. The feature is a useful way of presenting your case and establishing yourself as an authority in a particular field by virtue of working where you work. It is likely to present your organisation and your cause in a positive light. And you can always photocopy and distribute the article once it is in print. Send your news release to the Features Editor.

The Soft Story – these are articles which most frequently appear in the trash press like The Sun and The Mirror and in some magazines. They

---

The Centre for Alternative Technology is a registered charity and public limited company based in Powys in Wales. The centre aims to demonstrate renewable energy technologies, energy conservation and other aspects of alternative technology, e.g. organic food production. It also provides education and information for the public and has a membership.

The centre approaches the press by sending out news releases. The launch of the centre's £1 million share issue received publicity in the national press, whilst the construction of a water-powered cliff railway in Wales received coverage in the local press. The launch of the organisation's green guide to the local area received press attention both nationally and locally. The organisation has had little coverage in the tabloid press.

The organisation also promotes itself by taking out advertising space in tourist brochures, as the centre relies to a large extent on tourists visiting the area. This is a good way of "reaching the unconverted" and people are encouraged to attend courses.

focus on news items that have an emotional appeal. Be prepared to have your news release distorted so that the information is presented in a way which will almost certainly patronise the people whose cause your organisation represents, either through the language it uses or through the way it presents images. You will have to decide whether or not you are willing to put up with such coverage. If you are, send your news release to the News Editor.

The Photo Opportunity – you can often get your cause publicised through a good photo and caption. If you are organising an event, look at whether it is likely to provide a good "photo opportunity", e.g. somebody handing over a giant cheque or a celebrity participating in your event or in a stunt you have organised to bring your cause to public attention. This can be a valuable and inexpensive way to promote both your cause and your organisation.

Make sure you send the press a news release and invitation to the event well in advance and try to avoid arranging the event on a day when someone else is organising a major function. Always have someone from your own organisation taking photographs in case the press don't turn up. This will mean that you can send the photo with a news release about the event to those newspapers that didn't attend (most newspapers prefer large black and white photos). Even if there is no newspaper coverage, you can still use your photos in your own publicity materials.

Letters to the press – responding to an article by letter can be a good way of getting your viewpoint across and can help establish your organisation as an authority on a particular issue. Keep your letter concise and punchy (otherwise it will be edited down so that what you are trying to say may get a different slant). Your letter should usually be addressed to the Editor (or for a national broadsheet, to the Letters Editor).

Advertising space – buying advertising space can be a good way of having greater control over the message you want to get across. Prices tend to vary depending on the size of the ad and some magazines and newspapers carry free listings. Contact the Advertising Department or the Editor.

Radio

Local radio is another way of effectively reaching a local audience, often providing you with an excellent opportunity to discuss a sensitive issue. This may be through a magazine programme, or as a news story or through a phone-in. There are also community information programmes with details of forthcoming events and activities. There will be particular opportunities if there is a week-long or day-long stint

---

KEY POINTS

- ♟ Check that you are approaching the appropriate person

- ♟ Keep in touch with the reporter of your local newspaper

- ♟ Contact *all* the appropriate correspondents at a national newspaper

- ♟ Get your message across to the "unconverted"

of programmes addressing a specific issue.

As with the national press, national radio gives air time to stories that have a national angle, so unless your organisation has some news to report on that is likely to be of national interest and that accentuates a point recently made in the media, relates to new legislation or has something to say about a recent item of news, it may not be worth your while to approach national radio.

News Items – if your organisation has a strong story that is up-to-date and newsworthy, it is possible that someone from radio (either national or local) will follow up your news release by requesting an interview with someone in your organisation (often over the telephone). The interview may then be a part of a news item usually very heavily edited. For this reason, it is important to make a few main points rather than go into enormous detail. Try to practise what you are going to say before the actual interview if you can. Your news release should be sent to the News Editor.

Radio Features – find out about relevant programmes on the radio which could use your material for a feature. For example, your local radio station may have a regular community slot (approach the Community Affairs Producer to find out if such a slot is being planned and what the deadlines are). There may be slots on national radio specifically to give voluntary organisations air time.

A national radio station may also have programmes addressing a particular section of the community, e.g. "Women's Hour", "Does He Take Sugar" or "In Touch" on Radio 4. As well as this, there are now a number of radio stations specifically for minority groups (see Planning your media work, p.). Send your news release to the Editor of the programme or the Community Affairs Producer.

Radio Phone-Ins – you can often voice your opinion on an issue that might be brought up on a radio programme through a phone-in. This

---

KEY POINTS

☏ Approach local radio community information programmes and phone-ins to get your message across locally

☏ Approach programmes for minority audiences if you want to reach a specific audience

☏ Practice what you will say if you know you will be interviewed

---

ASRA Housing Association, a Leicester-based charity provides sheltered residential accommodation for elderly Asian people in the West Midlands. In 1993, Leicester Sound, the local radio station, interviewed the Chair of the management committee about the launch of a new housing development in Leicester, initiated jointly by ASRA Housing Association and Coventry Churches Housing Association. This coverage came about as a result of a news release and gave this small organisation a boost locally.

Anti-Slavery International is just one of the many organisations, which has promoted its cause on "The Week's Good Cause", a five-minute slot on Sunday mornings on Radio 4. Apart from giving Anti-Slavery International an excellent opportunity to raise awareness of issues around exploitation, this programme also brought in over £40,000 in donations.

is often less helpful if it is on a national programme, as it may not reach your target audience. However, all phone-ins enable you to get your message across and phone-ins on local radio can be useful if you are a local organisation trying to promote your cause in your area.

Television

Regional channels can address an audience within a specific geographical area, whilst national programmes can offer an organisation the kind of national public exposure it might be looking for.

Television News – as with radio, it may be possible to get coverage on the national news if your story is of major national significance or if it makes for an "And finally ..." soft feature. (Remember, soft features are often patronising in tone and likely to consist of a story with emotional appeal.) It is easier to get a regional news programme interested in your organisation. If your news release is of interest to the editor, you may be contacted for interview. Send the Editor of the appropriate news programme a copy of your news release.

Community Programme Features – there is often a community programme slot on regional television programmes. This can be very useful publicity for your organisation and cause because it can reach a local audience, often trying to address a specific issue of local concern and encourage participation in the community. Send your news release to the Community Affairs Programming Producer.

Documentaries – many of the documentary programmes are now made by independent producers, although some are still made in-house. You can try by keeping in touch with the producers by sending news releases. If they are planning a programme on an issue relating to your cause, they may then want to contact you. It is surprising how limited their experience and contacts in any particular field may be. Equally, you can target the Editor who will be considering which programme to commission, and your story might alert her to the importance of the issue.

SHELTER, a national organisation based in London, campaigns for decent affordable homes for everyone. It also provides assistance to people in housing need.

In 1993, SHELTER managed to get coverage through an interview with the organisation's director on a documentary about self-build accommodation. The programme was part of Channel Four's "Gimme Shelter" fortnight which addressed homelessness. Television coverage has done much to raise public awareness about the issue of homelessness and has dispelled myths about the work SHELTER does. It has also resulted in a few donations being made to the organisation.

Additionally, SHELTER undertook research for a First Sight documentary programme on squatting. Although SHELTER itself was not mentioned in the programme, it is likely that the programme-makers will remember the organisation and offer coverage another time.

SHELTER sends out news releases to documentary programme editors and journalists it has built up contact with and who are sympathetic to the cause. These are then followed up with a phone call. Carolan Davidge, SHELTER's Press Officer, says: "Organisations don't need expensive glossy news releases. Even local organisations can get national television coverage – they just need a well-written, simple, topical story with a human interest angle."

Magazine programmes – particularly throughout the morning there are hours of television programmes looking for items of interest to their viewers, e.g. "Good Morning". They reach a large audience and provide real and often undiscovered opportunities to get your message across. Send your news release to the producer of the appropriate programme.

Soaps – the ultimate for some causes is to get their message across in the storyline of a soap, such as "Eastenders" or "The Archers", for radio, which have an audience of millions. It is not impossible to get this kind of exposure but it may require considerable effort on your part. You should contact the Executive Producer of the series in which you wish your cause to feature, providing an imaginative outline of how your cause could be incorporated into the storyline. The outline should be no longer than one side of A4. More often than not, however, soaps such as Brookside or Eastenders, whose policy it is to take up causes, are likely to approach an organisation.

Discussion Programmes – these are often useful vehicles through which to stimulate debates on particular issues and can either be on a regional channel or national television. You could send your news release to Editors of programmes like "The Time... The Place..." and "The Crystal Rose Show" and others (see *Planning your media work,* below). who then may approach you to ask you to appear on the programme. You can ask to participate in programmes such as "Nation" or for tickets to "Question Time" when there may be the opportunity to ask a question or to add to the debate. Approach the producer of the appropriate programme.

Planning your media work

It is important that you plan all aspects of your media work. This will include keeping a record of contacts in the media and actively trying to establish good relationships with people working in the media.

Media contacts

Keep a list of all press and media contacts so that you can send them information on a regular basis. You can get names and addresses of press contacts as well as details about all the programmes, different journals, etc., from media directories, such as the *Pims Media Directory*, which is available from Pims House, Mildmay Avenue, London, N1 4RS, tel. 071-226 1000, *Benn's Press Directory*, available from Benn Business Publishing Ltd., Sovereign Way, Tonbridge, Kent TN9 1RW, tel. 0732 364422 or *BRAD* , available from Maclean Hunter, Maclean Hunter House, Chalk Lane, Cockfosters, Barnet, Hertfordshire EN4 0BU, tel. 081-975 9759.

For broadcasting contacts specifically, it is worth consulting both the Blue Book of British Broadcasting, available from Tellex Monitors Ltd., Communications House, 210 Old Street, London, EC1V 9UN, tel. 071-490 8018 and a television Factfile, available from the Independent Television Commission, 33 Foley Street, London, W1P 7LB, tel. 071-255 3000. Media directories are expensive, but are often

---

KEY POINTS

♥ Keep programme producers informed about your work by sending them news releases

♥ It is usually easier to get coverage on local television than on national television

---

The London-based **Alzheimers Disease Society** was approached in December 1990 by the production team of Eastenders for information about Alzheimers disease, so that a character with the illness could be introduced into the series. Clive Evers at the Alzheimers Disease Society's Information Department, considers the organisation's growing PR programme, (including its national awareness week) to have resulted in the Society's high profile in the media. "Organisations should be responsive to the media", states Evers, "Every opportunity should be treated with time, care and resources and organisations should have anonymous case studies and other information to hand." The Society's persistence with the BBC paid off and details of the Society's phone-line were advertised after each episode in which the character experienced particular difficulties. The actress, Edna Dore, who played the character, contributed by answering the first calls.

KEY POINTS

- ♀ Keep a list of press and media contacts
- ♀ Keep the media informed
- ♀ Make follow-up phone calls
- ♀ Try to establish a rapport

available at your local reference library. You can also try to borrow or get an old copy donated by a PR or advertising agency.

Good relationships with people in the media can be the key to getting media coverage. This is particularly so in the local media where people working in the media are more closely linked with the community. This involves keeping them informed about developments and new initiatives, inviting them to open days, presentations and launches of new projects. It is also very useful to keep in touch on the telephone by making follow-up phone calls once news releases have been sent out as the phone can often help establish a good rapport.

Setting up a PR system

by Becky Glenister, Sales and Publicity Officer, Charityfair

'Publicity' is the most useful word to describe how a small organisation spreads the word about its activities. In a large organisation there will probably be a marketing department and a separate public relations department working together. In a small charity, however, these two functions can be (and usually are) combined, and carried out by a single staff member.

There is a lot to be said for combining these two aspects of publicity. Being involved in a publicity drive from its conceptualisation through to witnessing practical results gives you a thorough understanding of the way your organisation is communicating with the public. This kind of overview is simply not possible in a large, cumbersome organisation. Inevitably, the fewer people involved in your publicity, the more control you have. You can decide what kind of publicity is appropriate – mailshots, press releases, flyers, posters, or newsletters. For small charities the line between PR and promotion is blurred and unimportant because you're fulfilling both roles.

Public relations – communication through the medium of the press and broadcast media – is just one tool you can use to get your message across. But...

■ What exactly is 'your message'?

■ Who are the people you are trying to reach?

■ What results are you looking for?

What do you want to convey?

You are closely involved in the day to day minutiae of your organisation's activities. The issues you are tackling will be firmly embedded in your mind. They will inform every statement you make, from every phone conversation you have to every letter you write. If you feel that up until now your publicity efforts haven't been getting you the results you need, and you haven't received the amount of press coverage you'd like, examine the way you are communicating. Can you convey what your organisation stands for in less than 50 words? Good PR means clear and accurate communication. You've spent days tracking down the feature writer of a magazine to persuade them to cover a story involving your organisation. Editorial in this particular publication would be of crucial importance to your campaign. You've finally got them on the line.... You've got 30 seconds to get their attention and raise their interest.

You cannot assume that everyone you come into contact with knows what you're talking about. You need to take time out to talk to colleagues and look at key issues. Putting into plain language what your organisation is trying to do is not necessarily an easy task. You need two or three sentences. The first to convey what your organisation stands for, the second to say what it does, the third sentence if appropriate, to explain what help is required. That in essence is 'your message'. A kind of mission statement which will provide a structure and fall back for all communication.

Charityfair, an annual three day exhibition for the voluntary sector, is organised by three people, one of whom is responsible for publicity. The Charityfair organisers wanted to promote the exhibition, and show what it was there to do. The following statement was arrived at:

'Charityfair is the major annual event for the voluntary sector. The exhibition is a chance for the whole voluntary sector to get together under one roof and say to the world at large "this is us, this is what we do, this is how you can help"'

Variations of this statement appeared in letters, press releases, bulletins and brochures. You can't hope to get across all the important issues which you are tackling in a single conversation or letter, but you can raise interest in what your organisation is doing, and leave an accurate impression of your objectives.

Who are you trying to reach?

Only you can know in detail who you want to make contact with. Broadly speaking you are publicising your organisation in order to attract support in the shape of funding or volunteers. Before you can find channels of communication which will reach potential supporters, you need to identify who they are. In the case of Charityfair one of the most complex parts of the publicity was attracting an audience for the Volunteering and Employment Forum:

'The Forum is aimed at members of the general public interested in working for a charity as a volunteer or paid employee. It offers practical advice in becoming involved in the voluntary sector in the shape of workshops, free leaflets, seminars and advice shops.'

The publicity for the Volunteering and Employment Forum needed to reach people who were looking for this kind of advice. In the early stages of planning the publicity, we identified about a dozen different groups of people who we felt should be informed about the advice on offer at the Forum. The groups included students, recent graduates, retired people and careers officers. The next step was to find out what publications they read, what television they watched and what radio they listened to.

The two major media directories PIMS and BRAD are a good place to start the research. All publications in the UK are listed from consumer magazines you'll find on the newsagent's shelf, to specialist 'controlled circulation' or subscription publications. Local newspapers are also included. All the local and national broadcast media are listed. The information about each publication or station includes the names of relevant feature editors. All entries are categorised according to the 'target group' they address.

The directories are expensive to buy. An annual subscription costs well over £200! Get hold of a copy through a library, and you can then begin to compile a press distribution list. Take your research a few steps further. Find out about other in-house publications and bulletins using your own contacts and include them on your press list. We asked all the Charityfair exhibitors to let us know about their newsletters so that the editors could receive regular press information about Charityfair. If you have received support from a local company, do they have a company newsletter or bulletin? Scour your library's notice board for local groups with newsletters or network magazines; can you link in with them and spread the word to their members about the work you are doing?

What results are you looking for?

Your objectives in publicising your organisation will be entirely dependent on your particular organisation's needs. However, one thing goes without saying, you'll certainly want more financial support. You might also need the help of more volunteers, be looking for more members, or be promoting a particular fundraising event you are organising. All of this adds up to the need for a generally greater awareness of your organisation, it's activities and it's needs. You are looking for editorial coverage.

There is more than one way to get editorial written or broadcast about your organisation. Save press releases for when you have something new to say – if you have a specific news story, an announcement, launch, new publication or you are launching a fundraising event. But you can make contact by phone with editors who cover your particular area in relevant publications, television or radio programmes on your press list. Say that you want to use their publication to reach a particular group of people, and tell them how your organisation is of relevance to their readers, listeners or viewers. Follow up phone calls with written information about your organisation.

When you are approaching a writer on a publication, it might be appropriate to put together a skeleton article for them to use. Or if you are talking to a busy editor, suggest that you write the whole article for them and submit it as a finished piece. Be aware that monthly magazines will be working about three months in advance of the date a publication hits the shelves, so if you want to appear in a May issue it's no good contacting a monthly in April.

Bigger is not necessarily better. Chasing national press and media coverage is often not worth the effort. Journalists are often difficult to pin down, and if you manage to interest them in a story, you can never guarantee what sort of coverage you will get, or indeed whether you will get any coverage at all. Refer back to the tightly focused areas of potential support you identified, and then concentrate on the publications that these people are reading or programmes they are listening to.

One important group of people for Charityfair to reach were Careers Officers. The best way to contact them was not to chase national newspapers for features on the career opportunities within the voluntary sector, but to get in touch with specialist publications like Career Teacher and Eurograd who immediately saw the relevance to their readers, and needed little persuasion to feature Charityfair.

Local is often better than national coverage. If no one in your locality knows about your existence this should be your first publicity push. You'll find regional newspapers and radio stations will be very interested in stories with a local angle, especially if you can organise an eye catching photo opportunity. If appropriate say how local people can help you, and be specific about the amount of money you need to raise, and the time you have in which to raise it.

PR can often be undertaken more effectively by smaller organisations than by the larger frequently more bureaucratic organisations. Never underestimate the value of good publicity and promotion. Done well, publicity and promotion can reinforce your organisation's credibility, help raise awareness of important issues and foster good links with the local community.

4 Building the credibility of your organisation

How your organisation is perceived, ties in to a large extent with the way in which you promote your cause. But there are a few things that you can do separately with the specific aim of enhancing your organisation's profile.

Presenting yourself: name and reputation

There may be things that you want to convey about your organisation, for example, that you are a lively group with lots of innovative ideas; or that you are a very "grassroots" kind of organisation, brimming with volunteer enthusiasm and local community involvement; or that you are concerned to find real long-term solutions to problems; or that you are a solid, consistent organisation with a track record of success; or that you collaborate effectively with other agencies. You will know what aspect you want to promote.

Here are a few things that can either contribute to the kind of image you might wish to convey, or detract from it.

Your organisation's name

It is important to think very carefully about the name you have chosen for your organisation. Does it say what you want it to say about you? What kind of ring does it have to it? Who does it sound like it's addressing? Do you want it to address that particular group of people?

Your name can describe succinctly the activities you undertake or the cause you are campaigning for. Names such as "Greenpeace", "WaterAid", "Friends of the Earth", "Landlife", "Shelter", "Parent Network", "National Peace Council", "Rural Voice", "Third World First" give people a picture of what the organisation is about in a very straightforward way.

Other names can describe your activities in a more indirect way, using words with a double meaning, e.g. "Bandaid" or "At Ease" (a

---

The **RNID** recently changed its name from the Royal National Institute for the Deaf to the Royal National Institute for Deaf People. What this change is saying about the organisation is that it is keeping in touch with its users and is "aware".

counselling service for members of the armed forces). If you go for this kind of name, you will have to be sure the double meaning or word play is understood by people outside your organisation. If the name you choose is a clever word play which is appropriate for your organisation, but which isn't instantly recognisable, then it is as well to add a short line following on, which explains the organisation's activities, e.g. "Re-Solv: Society for the Prevention of Solvent and Volatile Substance Abuse".

You can also use acronyms which can be a witty way of describing your organisation's activities. Again, unless these are blatantly obvious, these should be followed by the full name or an explanatory strap line, e.g. "WAR: Women Against Rape", "NIPPERS: National Information for Parents of Prematures: Education, Resources and Support". The danger of using acronyms, however, is that you can sometimes try desperately to fit the full name of your organisation to make an acronym that you find best suits you. This means that the full name of your organisation can end up sounding rather ludicrous! In such cases, it is probably better to abandon the idea of making your chosen name stand for the description of your organisation; instead add a sensible subtitle, e.g. "QUIT: The National Society of Non-Smokers.

If you just want to use a set of initials to represent the name of the organisation, you should again add a line of text about what you do. Never assume that your name will be recognised by other people just because you recognise it; unless your name spells out what you are about clearly and directly, it is wiser to lengthen your name, rather than risk people going "KLS who?"

Logos

Your organisation's logo goes hand in hand with your organisation's name. You may just want to use the name of your organisation without an accompanying symbol (a logotype). In this case, think carefully about the typeface (style of lettering) you use. What is it saying about your organisation? Who is it saying it to? Different typefaces can say different things about you.

If you want to use a symbol, make sure that it is well thought out. The symbol, like the name of your organisation needs to say something about what you do. For example, Save the Children Fund's logo is a child with outstretched arms. An image that is simple and makes a strong impact is often the best policy.

A lot of thought needs to go into your logo, as it will represent the organisation publicly and will remind people of your presence. It will also need to be one that works and that you will be able to use for some years.

Remember to take the people who use your organisation into account – you will not want to use a logo that undermines the people who use your services. For example, it could be argued that the Royal National Institute for the Blind's new logo of a person with a white stick continues to reinforce the stereotype of the disabled person as someone who is helpless and in need of pity and therefore perpetuates negative public perceptions.

Patrons

The credibility of your organisation can also be enhanced if you have a well-known patron or well-known patrons. Others will believe that if these people have lent their name to your organisation, they must have considered the organisation and its work important and worthwhile.

When you select a patron, make sure that the person you choose is genuinely interested in the cause. For example, someone who has a member of the family with the illness you are dealing with or someone with a personal concern for the issue you are working on. Someone who has themself overcome alcohol dependency, if you are an alcohol project, is more likely to help your cause than someone who has no connection or knowledge of the issues involved. Try not to approach a celebrity to ask for their patronage purely on the grounds of their being a celebrity – if they are going to reinforce your organisation's credibility, rather than damage it, they will have to be seen to be sympathetic to and interested in your cause and your organisation.

Sponsors

Sponsors can have a beneficial effect on the public image of your organisation in rather the same way that patrons can. If a well-known company or individual is supporting one of your projects, it is as well to make sure that people know about it. The fact that some have already supported your cause may attract others. Funders often feel that their own public image can be enhanced if their name is ranked alongside other "important" names. They may also feel that if someone "with a name" has supported the cause, it must be worthwhile.

You should make sure that the sponsors you choose fall in with the ethical stance of your organisation. It is worth drawing up guidelines for what support you will solicit and what you are prepared to accept and more importantly, what you are not prepared to accept because of the impact of that support not just on the public perception of your organisation, but also on how your service users, your existing supporters, your volunteers and your staff members will feel.

In addition, you will need to think carefully about the impact of a particular sponsor funding a particular project. For example, if you need sponsorship for a leaflet to advise people about treatments for an illness, it is probably unwise to have a drug company which produces drugs to

---

KEY POINTS

♟ Choose a patron who is likely to have a genuine interest in your cause and who will want to do something positive to help you

♟ Don't choose a celebrity, just because they are a celebrity

---

KEY POINTS

♟ Make sure people know about "important" names supporting your cause

♟ Sponsors should fall in with the ethical stance of your organisation

♟ Think about the impact of a particular sponsor supporting a particular project

> **TACADE** (The Advisory Council on Alcohol and Drug Education) is an organisation in Salford providing preventive education in the areas of alcohol and drug use. Its guidelines on support and sponsorship are fairly flexible and as long as the organisation's independence is not inhibited and its public image remains intact, TACADE is happy to accept support from most places. TACADE will not, however, accept support from companies operating in South Africa as this would be inconsistent with the organisation's equal opportunities policy. Nor will the organisation seek out funding from tobacco manufacturers, as its own stance is that no amount of tobacco is harmless. Yet it will accept support from drinks manufacturers, as TACADE's policy on alcohol is that responsible use is not harmful.

combat this illness to sponsor the production of the leaflet. However unbiased the work you do may be, it may not always appear that way to some people and could damage the name of your organisation.

Presenting yourself: image and impression

One of the most important elements in conveying an impression of a successful organisation is to maintain a good relationship with your supporters, whether they are service users, volunteers, funders or individual donors. Remember that every single contact with your supporters or with any member of the public conveys an impression of your organisation and its work. These people can become your ambassadors, telling others about your work and how good your organisation is – or the contrary if you create a poor impression. Creating a bad impression could mean losing someone who might otherwise be a valuable supporter.

But what do we mean by a "bad" impression? Nobody wants to support an organisation they believe will waste resources, run a shoddy service, fail to give value for money or to fulfil its objectives. So this is not an impression you will want to convey. Conveying the "right" impression or to put it another way, getting across a positive image of your organisation means that you will need to ensure that you function efficiently and effectively in relation to the people you deal with.

Contact on the telephone

When you speak to people on the phone, make sure that you sound efficient, that you either have the information they require or if you are unable to help them that you can refer them on to someone else in the organisation or to another organisation who will be able to help them. If you have the information they require, but it isn't at your fingertips,

KEY POINTS

- Make sure you sound efficient
- Prepare your phone calls in advance
- Refer people on if you cannot help them
- Answer people's queries promptly and effectively

The **South Essex Rape and Incest Crisis Centre** is an organisation whose public image is very much dependent on the way in which it responds to phone calls. It runs a crisis line for women who have been raped or sexually assaulted or who fear that they may be in danger of being raped or sexually assaulted. This means that people making calls to the organisation's crisis line are under a lot of stress and may find it difficult to deal with a delayed response. The Centre therefore tries to deal quickly and effectively with calls by operating a rota system and by ensuring that messages left on the organisation's answering machine are listened to at least once, if not twice daily.

The organisation's responses to general enquiries are met with the same level of efficiency, as it is important for the centre to be seen to be responding quickly, in order to persuade funders of its effectiveness. In fact, the organisation is well aware of the impact that a slow response can have on the public image of an organisation, as it constantly deals with local authority social services departments. Often social services departments take weeks to reply to a phone call resulting in a very negative public image and in the belief that local authorities are anonymous institutions.

then say you will ring them back, as it is always annoying to be kept waiting on the line. Make sure that you do then ring them back!

If you need to make contact with someone in another organisation to get information or to ask them to do something for you, prepare what you are going to say in advance so that you don't get tongue-tied. Always explain who you are and who you work for.

Contact through the post

All your letters to supporters should be well presented. This means they should be typed up clearly and neatly on a clean piece of paper. It also looks better if your letters are on headed paper (don't forget to quote your registered charity number on all your correspondence whether headed or not and on all your publicity material – this is now required by law). Publicity material should also be well presented. This doesn't mean that you have to come up with glossy brochures – in fact glossy brochures can convey the impression that an organisation is wasting money – but it helps if things are well laid out and are not smudgy or messy. Try to avoid typographical errors or spelling mistakes and as far as possible keep language jargon free.

Personal appearance and premises

You should be aware that how you and your staff present yourselves publicly makes an impact on what people think about the organisation. It is as well to think about this aspect, even if it is only to conclude that it is up to each person in the organisation to make their own decision. For example, if you make regular face-to-face contact with members

KEY POINTS

- Use headed paper
- Quote your charity registration number on all correspondence
- Make sure all written material is accurate and effective

of the public and service users, you may decide that you will want to look casually smart; you may want to take particular care with your appearance when you visit other organisations.

You might also want to think about how your premises looks, particularly if the public or service users visit your office. This may not necessarily mean you will want to invest in plush office furniture and flashy equipment, but it could mean clearing away floor spaces, making sure everything looks tidy and throwing in the odd potted plant. You may also want to consider how accessible your premises is to disabled people.

Briefing volunteers, staff and trustees

Another feature of an effectively run organisation is good communication. All volunteers, staff and trustees should be informed about the organisation's latest programmes and initiatives. They should know who within the organisation is able to deal with queries. All too often, people within an organisation fail to let other people know what is going on, resulting in great embarrassment when someone rings up to find out about, for example, "the new training initiative" only to receive the somewhat dismaying response "What new training initiative?". It is useful to have regular briefing meetings, or, failing that, memos could be sent around to let people know what is going on.

Effective financial management

Under the 1993 Charities Act, registered charities are required to keep regular accounts of their day-to-day finances. They must also have their accounts audited or examined independently. All registered charities are now obliged to state that they are a charity on all official documents and to produce a copy of their accounts if requested to do so by the public.

If you are a company limited by guarantee, you will be obliged to file your accounts with the registrar of companies. If you are an industrial and provident association, you will have to file your accounts with the registrar of friendly societies. Unincorporated associations, as the simplest form of legal structure, do not have to file accounts anywhere if they are not registered as charities, although it is always a good idea to keep accounts anyway.

Apart from fulfilling legal obligations, good financial management can help to enhance your organisation's credibility. Your accounts should be efficiently kept and you should be open and honest. Effective financial management will involve acting on your auditor's or the independent examiner's recommendations, implementing regular procedures for monitoring the organisation's financial health and keeping up-to-date with PAYE (if you employ staff on a full-time, part-time or casual basis) and VAT (if your turnover is sufficiently

---

KEY POINTS

- Bear in mind that personal appearance can make an impact
- Think about the way your premises looks

KEY POINTS

- Keep all staff and volunteers informed
- Hold briefing meetings
- Send memos about new initiatives

KEY POINTS

- Make sure everything is accounted for
- Be open and honest
- Act on your auditor's recommendations

high to require you to register for VAT).

You should ensure that there are no unexpected deficits, as this could drive you into insolvency. If you are accumulating surpluses of unspent cash, you may need to add a note to explain why this is happening and what you plan to do with the money. For advice about accounting consult your local Council for Voluntary Service or Charities Information Bureau.

Endorsements

Another way of contributing to the positive image of your organisation is to get other people to endorse your work, whether they are patrons, trustees, the press or your supporters. For example, use quotes from evaluation forms and questionnaires to enhance your standing in your publicity materials.

As well as this, make sure you keep copies of articles and photos in a cuttings file if you have managed to get press coverage, so that these can be used in publicity leaflets or in your annual report to lend credibility to your work. For broadcast items, try to record or videotape the coverage – you could then use these to promote your work at an open day.

KEY POINTS

- Get supporters to endorse your work
- Use good publicity to enhance your credibility

CASE STUDY

Gemma

Gemma, which was set up in 1976 as a collective, is a voluntary self-help group for lesbians and bisexual women with and without disabilities. Gemma has no paid workers and three volunteers. It publishes a national quarterly newsletter, runs a friendship network and an information service.

The general public's most common response to the organisation is one of incomprehension, whilst funders perceive the group more positively as a small self-funding voluntary group.

Although Gemma has no specific marketing strategy, its links with both the lesbian and gay and disability movements mean that the organisation successfully publicises its services in the lesbian and gay press, through disability organisations as well as in the media generally. The organisation's newsletter is also a useful tool with which to raise awareness.

Gemma does not have a specific fundraising strategy nor someone specifically responsible for developing this aspect of Gemma's work but that again does not mean that the job isn't done. Funds are raised primarily through group members, (there are around 200 nationally and about 6 outside the UK) and an annual income varying between £500 and £800 depending on the level of donations is generated. Small feminist and lesbian and gay organisations have also responded positively to Gemma and have been forthcoming with funding. However, Gemma recognises that the organisation's fundraising scope is limited. Says Coordinator, Elsa Beckett, "Mainstream companies would not be concerned with improving life for disabled lesbians, so there are only a small number of bodies we can apply to. This means that we make sure we do as much self-funding as possible, for example, by holding stalls at community events".

Gemma's main priorities over the next few years are to continue to produce its newsletter, maintain the friendship network and extend its outreach work to ethnic minority women. According to Beckett, members outside London are often deprived of a social life that is accessible. Gemma hopes to help remedy this by enlisting the active support of its members.

CASE STUDY

Gender Dysphoria Trust International

The Gender Dysphoria Trust International was established in 1981 to provide counselling, advice, support and information for transsexuals, their partners and families. Between 400 and 500 people use these services regularly and over 3,000 transsexuals or members of their family contact the trust each year on a one-off basis. The trust, a registered charity and a company limited by guarantee, is entirely dependent on volunteers of whom there are over twenty.

The organisation constantly needs to combat the public perception of transsexuals as "freaks" or "perverts", and its does so by presenting positive images of transsexuals in all publicity which is channelled through the media (press or television), via contacts with professionals, through leaflets and mailings to the transsexual community itself. The trust also promotes awareness of the issues around transsexuality by giving talks to medical groups, social workers, Samaritans and others.

Funders frequently perceive the organisation as being full of oddballs and the project has never received any government funding. However, this has not prevented the trust from implementing a fundraising strategy and stepping up its approach to grant-making trusts, in order to increase its £10,000 income which it currently receives through membership subscriptions. Whilst the project is realistic about its chances of success with the corporate sector – it is unlikely to approach companies whose attitude towards transsexuality is predominantly unsympathetic – the trust does not view tapping into corporate funds as an impossibility.

Over the next few years, the trust hopes to continue to promote positive images of transsexuals and to educate both the public and professionals. It also hopes to expand its currently limited services by employing staff and establishing a broader support network.

CASE STUDY

Legalise Cannabis Campaign

The Legalise Cannabis Campaign is a national pressure group, which was established in 1979, to provide educational material, an occasional journal, legal advice, local contacts and general information on cannabis. It also lobbies Parliament, MPs, trades unions, medical organisations and legal agencies and monitors media coverage of the issue. The organisation is run entirely by ten volunteers and has approximately 400 members.

In general the public perceives the organisation as having a membership of "idiots", "hippies" and "drug addicts", whilst funders consider the organisation to be a risky venture. Another obstacle is the fact that the organisation, as a group campaigning for a change in legislation is not entitled to charitable status and so can seldom meet the funding criteria of most trusts or companies. This problem is unique to small political campaigning groups and can be a major setback where funding is concerned. Says Geoffrey Cox, Secretary, "We don't know whom to ask for funding. Trusts and companies are unlikely to consider our campaign within their remit." For this reason the group is forced to rely largely on the funds it raises through its membership fees and fundraising stalls, which has generated an approximate annual income of £2,500.

Although publicity is relatively easy to organise, due to the number of people who are keen to promote the cause, publicity has tended to be quite low key and geared mainly towards the small press. For example, the group takes out paid advertisements in alternative magazines, such as Outlook, I.D. and Green Anarchist. It also keeps both the local and national media informed about the issue, although support from major publishers is often hard to get. Therefore, the campaign has to take advantage of other PR opportunities, e.g. publicity leaflets are handed out at events such as festivals, concerts, fairs, party political conferences, union conferences, at other campaigns and outside prevalent court proceedings. Much of the organisation's publicity, however, is done by word of mouth, a particularly successful method due to the fact that a ready-made network for communication has been established through the drug's illegal status.

Additionally, the campaign publicises itself abroad through like-minded campaigns, magazines and people. States Cox, "Foreign magazines and publishers are happy to mention us in exchange for a return mention." The campaign also has its own journal in which the organisation presents its case and which is often reviewed by other magazines.

PART THREE
Raising Money
& Getting Resources

This section looks at improving your chances of getting support by developing a fundraising strategy, preparing your approach to funders and making an application. It also has information on a few techniques for raising money and getting other support (such as volunteers) from individuals.

Articles are on "Making Assumptions, Making Grants" by Jo Habib, West Yorkshire Charities Information Bureau and "Volunteers and Good Practice" by Mark Rankin, Volunteer Centre UK.

Case studies in this section are on Belfast Law Centre, the Birmingham Settlement and the Hideaway Youth Centre.

1 Introduction

Whilst all promotion, PR and effective presentation can contribute towards persuading people to make a financial contribution, it is important to link these activities with good old-fashioned fundraising.

Effective fundraising doesn't just involve improving your applications to funders; it involves recognising the fact that an organised approach is the only way to be successful. Your fundraising strategy should be combined with careful research on appropriate funders.

It is also essential to recognise the value of "in kind" support, whether through secondments, equipment, training or volunteer support.

Additionally, you should be trying to win over the support of your local community, through organising activities in your area and making people aware of the work you are doing. This can lead to more money for your organisation and to committed support through volunteers.

Here is how to get to grips with the awesome task of making sure you get the resources you need.

2 Developing a fundraising strategy

If you are going to obtain the resources to put your long-term plans into practice, you will have to think about your fundraising strategy. Developing a fundraising strategy involves looking carefully at the work you are doing now and how this will change in the future. Do you hope to develop or expand current projects? What new projects do you expect to set up? Think at least three and possibly four years ahead. The longer you plan ahead, the more time you give yourself to raise the money. Planning should be an annual process. You can always amend your plans if circumstances change. Once you know what your plans are, it is a matter of establishing how much each new project will cost to run, and how much it will cost to continue to run your existing projects. Don't underestimate these costs. If your fundraising budgets are too low, you will end up in financial crisis. You will then be in a position to estimate the total amount you will need to raise over the next few years in order to be able to achieve your goals.

The next step is to implement your "fundraising strategy" and to work out how much you will try to raise from government grants and contracts, from grant-making trusts, from companies, from individuals through donations or fundraising events, etc. You need to start fundraising well in advance of when you actually need the money. Fundraising is an on-going process – if you start when the cash begins to dry up, then you will not only cause yourself and everyone else in the organisation a great deal of stress, but you may find that you are unable to raise the required amount in such a short period of time. Fundraising needs to be done continuously and at least one full year before you intend to use the money.

KEY POINTS

- Think at least three years ahead

- Work out how much you need

- Don't wait until you run out of money

3 Preparing your approach to donors

Before you actually get down to the nitty gritty of the application, you will have to do some research to find out which organisations and government bodies are worth approaching. It is a waste of time writing to organisations whose funding criteria could never in a million years have a bearing on your particular project. So find out who funds what and make a list of those funding sources that are relevant to your organisation. There are now lots of directories that can help you do this (see *Useful Publications*, page 119).

At the same time, however, look at your project closely. At first sight, your project may appear to be "unattractive" to funders. However, with a little imagination and creativity, it is possible for even the seemingly most "difficult" cause to match someone's criteria. For example, an organisation providing training for unemployed people could find a way to fit into the criteria of a trust making grants towards educational projects; an alcohol project providing counselling could try adapting their proposal to comply with the criteria of those giving grants or inviting bids for contracts for services in health and social welfare fields. Remember, also that there are ways in which funders can support you that don't involve cash – non-cash support can be just as helpful as money to a struggling organisation. Companies, for example, are often valuable as a resource for gifts in kind, secondments and training.

Community of the Peace People (Peace People), based in Belfast, Northern Ireland, is an organisation campaigning for peace and justice in Northern Ireland and carrying out social welfare activities such as youth work and work with prisoners.

The organisation receives funding for core costs from UK central government. However, Peace People would not approach government for support for its campaigning work or work with prisoners and young people as this could undermine the organisation's independence. The organisation therefore approaches charitable trusts with policies to support youth and peace work for funding towards these aspects of its work. Additionally, the organisation has links in the US through a support organisation which raises funds from US charitable foundations for the Community of Peace People's work. Because of the political nature of much of the organisation's work, companies are only ever approached for equipment.

KEY POINTS

- ? Make a list of poten-
  tial funders

- ? Match your project to
  the funder's criteria

- ? Know what makes a
  funder tick

- ? Think of non-cash
  ways in which a
  funder can help you

Once you have your shortlist of appropriate potential funders, you will have to start thinking about how you will make the approach. You will need to know what makes particular funders tick, for example, an approach to a grant-making trust would need to be different from an approach to a company. Different kinds of funders could therefore require the following different approaches:

- ◆ The grant-making trust – convince them that you are meeting a need, are an innovative project, that your project can be replicated elsewhere and that you run your organisation cost-effectively.

- ◆ The company – you will need to demonstrate to companies that they can themselves gain something from supporting your project, whether through educating their employees on issues of concern to you and to them, providing PR, or helping the company to form valuable links with the local community. You will also need to show that you provide value for money.

- ◆ The local authority – you will need to show local government that you are meeting a specific need within the local authority's remit, that you have effective ways of monitoring and evaluating your work, that you either have or are in the process of implementing an equal opportunities policy and that your services are run at a competitive price.

Your project proposal, then, will have a slightly different emphasis depending on whom you intend to approach.

4 Making an application to a funder

Whilst an appeal for funding is asking for something very specific, it can also function as an effective way of letting people know about your organisation and the way in which it works. A bad funding application not only doesn't get you a grant, but it also contributes to a negative image of your organisation in the eyes of that particular funding body. A good application, on the other hand, stands a better chance of success and promotes the reputation of the organisation. This could mean that although the application for a grant itself may not be successful, your organisation will be remembered for having put in a good application, rather than a bad one. This can help promote both the organisation and the cause – and you may be successful next time.

A good application meets the criteria of the funding body and is addressed to the correct person. It should consist of a covering letter, a project proposal, a breakdown of costs and supporting literature about your organisation.

Your **covering letter** should briefly:

- outline the need for the project
- state why the funder should make a grant to your organisation
- say how much is required in total
- state how much you are requesting from them
- say who else you have approached
- state how much you have already raised

Your **project proposal** should provide details about:

- the need for the project
- the objectives of the project
- how you will go about meeting this objective
- the specifics of the actual project itself
- the timescale of the project
- the expected outcomes and how you will measure success

The **accompanying costing** should give a breakdown of all the costs which will need to be met if the project is to go ahead, including things like electricity, postage, staff costs, management costs, etc. If you are applying for a capital project (for a building or equipment), then you

---

KEY POINTS

- ☛ A good application can help promote the reputation of an organisation
- ☛ Applications should give full details of the proposal
- ☛ Applications should be concise and well-presented

may need to show how the running costs are to be met. If you are applying for a large sum, you will need to show how you plan to raise the rest. If you are applying for short-term funding (one or even three years) to run a long-term project, you will need to show what you propose to do when the grant runs out. All this information should be well-presented, concise and accessibly written.

✒ Making Assumptions, Making Grants

by Jo Habib, West Yorkshire Charities Information Bureau

Despite the voluntary sector's overt concern for equality, access and diversity, stereotyping is alive and well in many areas of voluntary action; the funding arena is no exception. One reason is time. For many grant-makers, time's winged chariot provides constant background noise. The grant cycle rolls inexorably on, the pile of applications threatens to overwhelm the administration, and the cost of bringing together decision-makers never diminishes. So the search is on for ever more efficient (read speedier) decision-making processes. This means that the temptation to make assumptions, to use mental short-hand, is great.

"A self-help group? I know what that means." "A minibus appeal? I already know the arguments for and against." "AIDS? I know about AIDS." "That part of the country? It's wealthy." "That minority group? They have these characteristics ..." Just to get through the workload, funders make assumptions. And part of a grant-seeker's task may be to challenge them.

But if funders stereotype, so do grant-seekers. "Funders are conservative." "Funders are conventional." "Funders are English, white, middle-class, middle-aged men." Indeed many are. But even white men in suits differ from each other. Businessmen may be pacifists (think of the companies headed up by Quakers), trustees may be gay, councillors may have been abused when young.

Hence, the standard funding maxim, **Do Your Homework**. This is often easier said than done. If the funding body is local, you can ask around and see if anyone has had money from it or if anyone recognises the names of the trustees. But that may well be it.

If you have more information to go on, look carefully at the language the funder uses. Is it politically aware, old-fashioned do-gooding, carefully considered, vague enough to be a smokescreen for funders' whims, or what? If there are lists of past grants, what does that tell you about the kinds of groups or activities they might support? Are their interests wide or focused? Funders that have clear, specific interests tend to have considerable expertise in the area in question – talk down to them at your peril.

If they're a company, a quango or statutory agency, or the kind of charitable trust that welcomes preliminary enquiries (usually trusts with staff), it may be worth phoning them before you apply formally. What you're trying to do is get a feel for them, get an idea of where they're coming from, what makes them tick.

Many groups research into funders very effectively but still don't get money. Why is this? If funders are not all alike, why does such a small proportion of charitable income go to "unpopular", "unglamorous", "difficult" causes? Partly its just semantics. "Difficult" causes are by definition those which receive little funding. The point to remember here is that things change; today's difficult cause may be tomorrow's bandwagon. Over the last decade overseas aid has yo-yoed, environmental issues probably peaked at the end of the eighties, while poverty – despite the ever-widening gap between rich and poor – has not managed to be flavour of any month. So one long term strategy to increase grant-aid is to popularise your cause, get it on the public agenda and legitimise it in the eyes of funders. There's a certain amount of chicken and egg involved – the easiest way of legitimising a cause is to have someone put significant money into it. Nevertheless there are a variety of ways of raising the profile of an issue.

Some work, however, is difficult to fund not because the cause is out of fashion but because of the level at which the work is taking place. "Ordinary" community-based voluntary action – the playgroup, the sufferers association, the youth club, the local campaign, the refuge, the drop-in centre, the local development agency – may not be contentious or unpopular but may rather fall into that big black hole called Others Should Fund.

Think of it from the funder's point of view. They have limited resources. They have high ideals. They want to make their grants work, have impact, make a difference. There's great demand, they can't fund everything. How do they select?

One way is to support initiatives which have a finite term. Fund for three years and no more and the money becomes available again; fund on an open-ended commitment and the money's tied up forever – grant-makers have done themselves out of a job. Another is to decide, as a policy, not to provide core-funding. This used to be a line taken by trusts and companies – "statutory sources fund the bread and butter work, we provide the jam" – but is now increasingly adopted by statutory agencies, too, who maintain they don't wish to encourage dependency.

There are a variety of other ways in which funders manage to say, "We don't do that." Sometimes it's just tradition, unwritten rules. Sometimes there are clear guidelines, periodically reviewed. Whether vague or precise about their criteria, however, funders are likely to favour initiatives which at least seem to promise to be a catalyst or demonstrate what's sometimes called the "multiplier effect". This means that the grant can be used to lever or attract other money. In a similar sort of way, the ubiquitous desire to fund "innovative" projects is an attempt to get more value for money; fund the first kind and you can almost take the credit for all the replicated projects that follow from it.

Finally, and perhaps most crucially, funders are more likely to choose projects that are "well thought out", plausible and likely to work, rather than projects which are high risk, don't hang together, or are "well-meaning but woolly". They will be looking for a track record (can these people actually deliver?), for internal consistency and realistic costing in the proposal (have these people asked for enough?), and above all for clarity – what's the problem? how can it be tackled? how will anyone know whether things have got better? Funders want to fund success.

If that's the picture from a funder's perspective, what are the implications for a grant-seeker?

To begin with grant-seekers need to assess how likely it is that a given funder will say, "This is not for us, it's for someone else to fund." If this *is* a likely response, why exactly will the funder try to pass the buck?

Whatever kind of group you are, don't ask yourselves, "Why should these people be interested in funding *us*". Instead, ask, "Why should these people be interested in funding *the work we want to do*?" Check that the emphasis of your appeal is on the ultimate beneficiaries. In every case there ought to be a reason "out there" in the real world, something other than "our organisation will be damaged if we don't get money". Demonstrate, for example, that people are being exposed to dangerous pollutants, or are unable to participate in the life of their community (and are therefore suffering), or whatever it is. You need to show that the proposed work can make a difference to a real, tangible problem and that it falls within the funder's criteria.

If your case is hard to get funding for because it's "unpopular" or specialised, you may suspect funders will say to themselves, "these beneficiaries do not 'deserve' help", or "these people are not part of 'our' community" and are therefore "not our problem". You can either challenge their assumptions or deliberately use language you know will resonate with and not antagonise the funder.

If you think the funder will recognise that your appeal falls within their remit but will reject it because your work is not special or exciting enough, look around for additional reasons why they in particular should or could be interested. Such reasons might be:

- our work is initially unlikely to attract funding locally; we need start-up support from a far-seeing, risk-taking, pioneering body like you in order to demonstrate its value;

OR

- we're addressing the problem locally, you're interested in local causes; *and/or*
- we need support from you in order to gain credibility with other funders.

There may be other ways in which you can suggest that their money will go further – be more productive than usual.

- Is your project of more than local significance?
- Might there be matching money from somewhere else?
- Could your work be a model for others?
- Could you cascade your experience down?

If so , are you prepared to build the "added value" element into your work?

What if you believe funders will reject you because you're looking for core funding? If the answer to the question, "Do we look like we'll be forever dependent on this funder?" is yes, there are two ways of proceeding. One is to acknowledge the fact, one is to try to disguise it.

Acknowledging the fact, which is only likely to be effective with statutory funders, means taking one of two lines. One is:

"Realistically, you're the only agency that's going to fund the bulk of the work we do. But you ought to be (or are required to be) concerned about the issues we're tackling, and 'buying' us to do the work is more effective than doing it yourself."

This is the contract culture approach – no one says that day centres are unhealthily dependent on statutory support, even if 100% of their core costs are paid by the authority. The other line is:

"Realistically, you're the only agency that's going to fund our core costs. But if you do that, we can bring in to the area all sorts of additional resources because of project work we'll undertake/we'll create all sorts of inward investment because we'll add value to the area/our activities will generate employment opportunities, so actually it's very cost-effective to support us."

Disguising the fact of dependency usually means packaging up a long-term initiative into short-term chunks or being extremely optimistic about the future. Being optimistic could be, "By the fourth year our project will be self-sufficient", or, "We have every reason to believe that the health authority will provide core funding once the value of this approach has been demonstrated." Expect a degree of cynicism from funders if you take this approach.

Packaging up is to turn core costs into a string of projects, to say, "We are looking to fund the work initially for three years. There will be a full evaluation and the results will inform future developments". After the three year period, another three-year project, "building on the lessons learnt" is proposed. The drawbacks of this approach are obvious but many groups adopt this strategy as the only realistic way to get core funding.

Finally, ask yourselves, "What assumptions are we making about these funders?" Are the assumptions justified or are you stereotyping? You may not know much about them, so you may have to guess what they're like. But whatever you do, never underestimate a funder.

5 Raising money and getting support from individuals

When it comes to raising money and getting other support from individuals, all your work promoting your cause and your organisation will hopefully reap financial rewards. (See *Promoting your cause and your organisation*, page 36) However, there are a number of specific techniques, particularly at local level, that you can use to try to encourage individuals either to dig into their pockets or to become involved as a volunteer, or, if you're lucky both.

The first step in fundraising and recruiting support locally is to organise a local committee. This can be made up of staff from the organisation and volunteers who already support you from the local community, who are prepared to commit themselves to your cause. This could mean asking local contacts to help and finding out whether their particular skills could be of use to you.

There are numerous activities that you can undertake locally – from the garden fete to the car boot sale. Here are a couple of tried and tested ways of getting support from the public.

Sponsored events

This is an excellent way of raising the awareness of a large number of people and getting them involved in your organisation. You will have to decide what kind of activity your members would be interested in. Sponsored events take quite a lot of planning – you will need to make sure that you plan routes if you are organising a sponsored cycle ride or walk, print publicity materials, organise volunteers to help at the event, arrange for the collection of the sponsorship money (it is useful to keep a register of those who are getting sponsors). Your sponsorship forms should also be carefully thought out with enough space for people's names and addresses. You may also need to arrange for insurance cover.

Door to door collections

Unless your organisation has been granted exemption by the Charity Commission (this usually applies to the larger organisations organising national collections), you will need a permit from your local council. The council will want full details of the planned collection, so work all this out in advance.

> ## KEY POINTS
>
> ☛ Plan carefully
>
> ☛ Keep a register of sponsors
>
> ☛ Design effective sponsor forms

KEY POINTS

♀ Get permission from
the local council

♀ Brief your volunteers

♀ Make sure volunteers
carry a permit

The usual way of collecting door to door is to drop in an envelope for the donation together with a covering letter outlining the work of the organisation and how it meets needs (see *Presenting your case*, page 31). This would normally then be followed up by a visit from a person collecting the donation a few days later.

People collecting on your behalf should be well briefed and should carry a permit from your organisation allowing them to collect for you.

Street collections

You will need a licence for this – apply to your local council as above. It is important that you choose an appropriate location, i.e. one where there are likely to be a large number of people passing by, like shopping centres, high streets, etc. Try to instil a positive attitude into your street collectors and make sure you have a sealed collection box as well as any leaflets to hand out about your organisation.

KEY POINTS

♀ Think about the
location

♀ Make sure collectors
have a positive
outlook

These are just a few examples but there are a multitude of techniques that you can use to raise money from the public. The most important aspect of organising any fundraising bash is to plan well in advance, think carefully through everything that needs to be done and brief the people involved.

The **Caring and Sharing Trust** in Northamptonshire provides help and support for people with learning difficulties, particularly for those living in rural areas.

The trust organises a range of different local fundraising activities including auctions and Christmas parties for the police force. The organisation is spared most of the costs as everything from the night club to food is donated. Its patron, Suzannah York, also plays a major role in persuading people to give their services free of charge.

6 Developing and maintaining relationships

An important element of any fundraising plan is your ability to develop and keep mutually beneficial relationships with those who support you, whether through donations, volunteer involvement or gifts in kind. Personal relationships are the key to improving your prospects. You can do this by inviting funders and individual supporters to any events that you organise and by keeping in regular contact with them. It is also important to maintain links with them.

Feedback

This is a very important part of raising or maintaining a good public profile and unfortunately it is a side which frequently gets neglected. It is essential that you show supporters that they are appreciated. Too often, charities are so busy trying to scratch around for funds that they forget that people who have supported them in the past, may well help out again, if only they didn't feel that the organisation they were supporting was operating on a purely "money-grabbing" basis.

A letter of thanks or a phone call for an individual donation (no matter how small or insignificant the donation may seem to you) will show someone that you appreciate their support and might encourage them to help you again. Similarly, volunteers need to feel that the work that they do has not been taken for granted.

Any other feedback that you can give also helps to forge your relationship with your supporters and enhances your profile in their eyes. For example, in your letter thanking a supporter, you might also mention what their contribution went towards – describe the project that the individual's donation helped to set up, or say how their contribution towards the salary of an extra counsellor will benefit clients. All feedback should relate the supporter's donation or other support to the benefit to the people who use your service. It is very important that you make this link – people will want to know how their support is making a difference to the people your organisation was set up to serve. It is also worthwhile keeping your supporters up-to-date about developments in your organisation – make them feel involved and appreciated.

Likewise, all grants and donations from grant-making trusts and companies should be acknowledged as soon as possible with a letter

> ### KEY POINTS
>
> • Thank your supporters
>
> • Let them know how their money was spent
>
> • Comply with funders' reporting requirements

of thanks. Note the reporting requirements which may be a condition of the grant and make sure you comply with them. You will also want to report back on the particular project that the funder has supported, demonstrating your effective use of the funds and what you have achieved. Where you receive a grant from a statutory authority, the same applies (although with contractual arrangements becoming the predominant means by which an organisation is funded, your relation with the authority is likely to be much more formal from the outset).

✎ Volunteers and Good Practice

by Mark Rankin, Head of Training and Development, Volunteer Centre UK

No management process can be entirely objective in its approach. Any proposed system will carry with it the ideas and attitudes of those proposing and implementing a particular management structure. Inherent in any process of managing people are ideas and feelings about authority, status, relationships, priorities, benefits and objectives, all of which have strong subjective elements to them. It will never be possible to suggest some universal management system appropriate to the whole spectrum of voluntary work. But it is critical that any service involving volunteers has a comprehensive support system for volunteers.

Creating that system means an organisation must be clear and honest about its reasons for involving volunteers. For example, how seriously should we take a statutory department which affirms its belief in volunteers and then appoints a volunteer organiser with less status than most of the paid workers? Or fails to invest in training its paid workers in volunteer involvement? What kind of double message is given to the volunteers about the attitude of the organisation and the way it values volunteers?

A system of good practice in working with volunteers will vary from organisation to organisation depending on what resources are available and the nature of the organisation's task. However, any sound system of management and good practice will have a number of themes in common:

- values
- resources
- equal opportunities
- mutuality

These themes act as a strand which runs throughout the process and binds a good practice system into a comprehensive whole. Good management structures combine elements which are mutually reinforcing and reflect a consistent approach to the management task. For example, the gap between management expectations of its workforce and standards of behaviour set by managers has frequently undermined credibility and demotivated the workforce. These attitudes have often been carried over from managing the paid workforce to managing volunteers. A management process should seek to remove internal contradictions.

Values

Managing volunteers is a value laden exercise and is recognised as such when it comes to the management of paid staff. A value based approach to the management task is different from one which assumes that doing the task is all that matters and volunteers can simply be "used" as a means to that end. Instead, it is a powerful motivator for volunteers, generating loyalty and commitment from paid and unpaid workers.

Few potential volunteers respond to straightforward public appeals for help. One reason for this may be that organisations spend too little time on getting across to the public what they stand for and what their values are. Organisations do not generally project their identities but focus instead on the task or cause. Although potential volunteers can be motivated through altruism, many are also looking for an organisation that they can feel part of and can identify with. These days, there are many organisations working in the same fields competing for volunteers. The successful recruiters are those organisations which not only describe the need, but which can also convey a clear identity and the values they stand for in their recruitment message.

As for support, volunteers frequently do not feel sufficiently valued. If an organisation does not have its own value base then it is quite probable that volunteers will be treated as units of labour with little recognition given for their worth or their achievements. A value based approach is therefore an integral part of any management structure, reinforcing good working relations and enhancing the benefits both to the volunteer and the organisation.

Resources

Resource investment is an exercise in costing and prioritising aspects of the structure according to the values of the organisation. You will need to decide what resources are available and how much you can invest in involving volunteers. There are no zero costs in voluntary activity and you should not attempt to manage volunteers on the cheap. However scarce resources may be, the important task is to identify the ideal structure and then to establish the kind of resource investment required. The costing exercise will give a realistic idea of the total cost of a volunteering policy and reveal the gap between available and required resources. It is important to prepare a budget based on a detailed policy and to seek the necessary resources to implement that policy. Secondments and giving in kind are examples of how local businesses can help with the management task.

Equal Opportunities

An equal opportunities approach to recruitment includes making the message accessible to a wide range of groups represented in a particular community. This means knowing of their existence by conducting some initial research and understanding what makes it easy or difficult for certain groups to respond to a recruitment campaign and tailoring your campaign to take their needs into account.

An equal opportunities approach to recruitment also means not relying on word of mouth particularly if your existing group of volunteers is not representative of the local population no matter how successful this method may be. Remember that 72% of volunteers are managerial or professional workers and that 80% of volunteers were in full time education until at least age 21. Volunteering is the preserve of one section of the population. In order to challenge this, any equal opportunities approach to selection needs to emphasise a person's potential as much as their actual skills and experience. This can be achieved through both the volunteer and the organiser constructing their own job description and person specification. This allows a greater exploration of how both parties may best benefit from the planned relationship.

This approach requires more work from the organiser – interviewing skills are particularly important since more negotiation is required than in the cut and dried situation of fitting people into specified jobs. However, the organisation benefits by maximising the potential of people by recognising an individual's capacity for growth and development.

Additionally, an equal opportunities response to support emphasises flexibility and tries to accommodate the needs of the widest possible range of volunteers. This requires an organisation to acknowledge that people's needs and motivations vary and that once in the voluntary post, a person's motivation may change as their needs are met. Some people may not want any support at all, but others will want a great deal of support if they are to gain confidence through their work.

Mutuality

Good practice places an emphasis on an equal and complementary partnership between volunteers and their organisations. By enabling volunteers to maximise their potential through providing a choice of work and appropriate support and by giving recognition, the organisation will benefit from volunteers who are committed and motivated and who will contribute to the better functioning of the organisation.

This approach is different from the one which excludes volunteers from the decision-making processes and focuses on control rather than mutuality. The "controlling" organisation deprives itself of valuable feedback about its own performance. Mutuality is a value which should be made explicit as part of an organisation's value base and should be expressed through a written agreement outlining the rights and obligations of both the volunteer and the organisation. The agreement provides the basis for the relationship between the volunteer and the organisation and is the benchmark against which everything else is tested. Without such an agreement there can be no adequate organisation of volunteer effort since there is no sense of those mutual rights and obligations which are the usual basis for working relationships. Contracts and job descriptions are standard for the paid workforce and should be for volunteers as well. Along with establishing both parties' obligations and rights, the agreement reinforces the organisation's commitment to good practice.

Mutuality signifies an equal and complementary partnership between volunteers and organisations. Such mutuality can only come about if volunteers are empowered and have the confidence to operate as equal partners. This approach to empowerment needs to be made explicit and expressed in a written agreement. It is this agreement which usually holds the entire management process together and provides the basis for the joint relationship.

CASE STUDY

Belfast Law Centre

Belfast Law Centre helps advice agencies to inform people of limited means of their legal rights and to establish those rights. It gives advice and undertakes casework for people who are referred to the centre. It also provides a training and information service for advice workers and takes on development work to support advice agencies. The centre has a central office in Belfast and an area office in Derry to cater for the whole of Northern Ireland. There are around 21 paid staff, six of whom are temporary and between four and eight volunteers.

The project's annual income amounts to approximately £380,000, 90% of which comes from central government, 5% from local authorities and grant-making trusts and 5% from membership and training fees, legal aid and sales of publications. The organisation is only beginning to approach non-statutory funders although it perceives its services as an area which should be funded mainly by central government. Private funders are therefore only approached for contributions towards very specific projects and capital items.

As far as publicity is concerned, the organisation is faced with the dilemma of being unable to deal with the number of clients that PR on a large scale generates. It therefore only publicises its services to selected groups by leafleting and via the local media. It has managed to maintain good relations with funders, who are aware of the centre's broad range of political support. The accountants Price Waterhouse have also recently given the law centre a positive review which has contributed towards endorsing the organisation in funders' perceptions.

The centre fears, however, that cuts in legal aid could lead to an increased and unmanageable workload and that they will have to continue to operate without an increase in funding. However, Belfast Law Centre hopes to expand its service with solicitors and caseworkers to cover areas outside Belfast and to establish a capital development fund to purchase premises.

CASE STUDY

The Birmingham Settlement

One thing the Birmingham Settlement certainly doesn't suffer from is a lack of credibility. Set up ninety four years ago, its strength comes from the way it manages to combine running projects of national significance, like its National Debt Line, with its strong local tradition as a Birmingham charity.

The Settlement brings together support services for people in need and innovative proactive projects searching for new ways to tackle debilitating social problems. This has the added advantage of raising the organisation's national profile and strengthening its ability to attract extra funds for its "less appealing" services. The National Debt Line, pioneered by the Settlement in the 1980s, shows how the Settlement uses local social welfare problems as a springboard for raising issues nationally. The Line was originally set up to help advise the many people who were suffering the effects of the 80s credit boom. Other national initiatives include the Poor Man's Lawyer Service, the Right to Read Campaign and Fuelsavers' Helpline.

Recent fundraising successes have involved matching private sector funding with services. The Fuelsavers' Helpline is being run in partnership with British Gas, whilst the highly successful National Debt Line was originally given annual funding of £33,000 by the Department of the Environment, the parent of the project. However, when this was abandoned because the Department of the Environment's funding priorities changed, it was rescued by the Retail Credit Group with a grant of £70,000 and then taken on by the Money Advice Trust. Now, some of the Settlement's activities actually generate a surplus, including the publications, money advice training and the Settlement's research consultancy.

However, fundraising is never complete, particularly as the Settlement is determined to become independent from government funding – potential funders will be lobbied with a vengeance. Says Barbara Welford, part-time fundraiser for the organisation, "We don't want to be slick, gimmicky or glitzy, but we do want to be forward thinking and professional. We have to rid ourselves of that 'mend and make do' philosophy".

The two main factors which now appear to ensure the long-term viability of the Settlement are that it has become a household name in Birmingham and that it now has a proper donorbase. However, it was a long time coming, as Welford explains, "For eighty five years we had no idea who had supported us."

CASE STUDY

The Hideaway Youth Centre

The Hideaway Project is based in the Moss Side area of Manchester, which is so often the focus of negative media attention. The centre, which was set up for young Black people, sends out more positive images and provides vital services in an area marked by poverty and social deprivation.

The Hideaway Youth Centre was built following a successful capital appeal for £170,000. £40,000 of the total was provided by the Department of the Environment, which was persuaded to increase its original offer of £25,000. Local businesses have also provided a fertile source of funding – a sensible move, as the businesses who give support are not only getting good PR for themselves but are also ultimately investing in the area where they are based, boosting their own business prospects.

The size of the appeal at no time daunted the fundraisers – they were convinced of the need for the project to help ensure young people were exercising their full rights and knew what their responsibilities were – it was not a case of getting access to a table tennis table or a swimming pool. This means that the Hideaway Youth Centre works to make sure young people are given their rights in prison and that they get the welfare rights they are entitled to. Solicitors are also encouraged to do more.

Hartley Hanley, who coordinated the most recent large capital fundraising appeal, feels that although the Centre is of huge importance to the Black community, it is also there to benefit white working class people and elderly people. Work with all these communities helps towards promoting community strength.

Hanley feels that Black organisations need to collaborate to improve their chances of getting funding. "At the moment, Black groups simply compete against each other for scraps", he states. Many large organisations which do not specifically cater for Black people, but which may be developing projects aimed at this community are applying for funds allocated specifically for projects for Black people. This means that competition is intense and that small Black projects are losing out to large mainstream charities, that are not Black-led. By organising Black groups into collective bodies, Hanley is confident that this imbalance can be rectified.

PART FOUR
Ways of doing better

It is important to be aware of some of the difficult situations that you may come across, so that you can address issues and move forward. This section looks at the possible dilemmas involved in fundraising and promotion and suggests ways of overcoming them. There are also a few other suggested strategies for improving the way you work.

An article, "Networking to Promote your Cause" by Vijay Krishnarayan, NCVO looks in more detail at the way in which organisations can tap into resources by liaising with other organisations.

Case studies focus on the Naz Project and Prisoners Abroad.

1 Introduction

So we've established that enhancing your profile and raising money are necessary activities for any successful organisation. However, neither of these activities come without certain problems and ethical dilemmas.

These dilemmas are often part of the reason why people may be reluctant to look more closely at their publicity and fundraising. Some of the difficulties which may arise could revolve around trying to decide on time and resource allocation for fundraising and publicity; running the risk of going against the principles of your organisation; competing with other voluntary organisations for resources; and setting up projects purely to secure funding. You can in fact improve the way you work by looking at ways of dealing with such problems. Here we give you some suggestions.

Obviously publicity and fundraising are not the only things that need to be taken into account. Here are a few other ideas and strategies which could enhance the way your organisation functions. Acknowledging your role within the voluntary sector, planning well in advance, building a strong management committee and making sure that you tap into all the possible funding sources can all contribute to the continued success of your organisation.

2 Possible dilemmas and how to cope

Trying to promote your organisation and raise money does not come without problems. This will mean that you will have to look at *how* you are undertaking these activities. Often you can solve these problems by ensuring that raising your profile and fundraising are not done in isolation. They should be tied in with other aspects of your work.

How much time and money should you spend?

Once you have acknowledged the fact that profile-raising and fundraising are important, you may find allocating adequate time and money for these activities a problem. You will recognise that service provision is your main objective (so most of your resources should be ploughed into delivering the service) but in order to continue to resource the work you do, you will need to raise money and enhance your public image.

The best way of dealing with this is to consult your colleagues and management committee so that you come up with a budget and time allocation that people in the organisation feel comfortable with. Remember that the promotion and fundraising that you will be able to do is dependent on the level of resources which are available. You may decide that your organisation can afford and could benefit from a major publicity and money-raising campaign. To do this, you will either need to allocate parts of your income for this and employ someone to undertake the campaign or you will need to raise money specifically for this purpose. Or you may feel that a small boost to your publicity material is all that is needed at the present time, or that this is all that your financial situation allows for; in which case, only a small amount of money will need to be allocated and you'll be able to incorporate the work into someone's current work programme.

Never try to bite off more than you can chew or you will find yourself coming unstuck. But it is important to recognise that you may need to do something. As a guideline, you might decide to spend 2.5% -5% of your time and resources on promotion and external relations and 5%-10% on fundraising.

In fact, you should guard against overdoing your publicity. If you are seen to be spending too much on publicity or promotion, your supporters might start wondering where their money is going. Doing too much publicity might not just mean neglecting your service users, but it could conceivably be detrimental to the public image of your organisation. You might be seen to be talking too much and doing too little. It is the quality and effectiveness of your work which gives you the right to promote your organisation. Striking the right balance is very important.

Below is a list of things you might want to take into account, when deciding how much time, money and effort you will want to spend on promoting your organisation and raising money.

◆ Do people within your geographical remit know who you are?

◆ Is the level of support (both financial and volunteer) you are getting increasing, stable or decreasing? If it is decreasing, you have a problem which needs to be addressed urgently. Promotion and publicity may not be the complete solution; you may need to do some market research to discover whether there is an underlying more fundamental problem. If it is increasing, you may still want to do more; since you are attracting support, it may be sensible to "go for it" while the conditions remain favourable.

◆ How much can you afford to spend? Have you budgeted for this expenditure or will you need to raise extra resources for this?

◆ Can someone take on the publicity work as part of their current work programme?

◆ Or will you need to employ someone else to do the work?

The **Council for the Advancement of Communication with Deaf People** (CACDP) in Durham promotes training in communication skills to enable hearing people to communicate with deaf people. It also operates an examination system in these skills.

The CACDP has one paid member of staff who undertakes fundraising, PR and publicity activities. Regular reviews of the organisation's work ensures that the right amount of money is allocated for publicity and fundraising. At present, 5% of CACDP's total budget is allocated for these activities.

The kind of publicity and fundraising that the organisation undertakes is fairly modest. It never undertakes "cold" mailings, but always tries to send out publicity and appeal letters to people and organisations with whom it has had some contact, e.g. students who have taken the organisation's exams. It also makes appeals to companies and specific grant-making trusts for project funding. Because of the organisation's low-key approach, accusations of wasting resources on publicity are never made against the organisation. Ruth Holmes, Fundraiser and Publicity Officer at CACDP says, "Organisations shouldn't feel they can't spend some money on publicity and fundraising. It is always worth starting with those organisations you already have links with".

The risk of compromising your cause

When you decide to take on the task of promoting your organisation, it is all too easy to get carried away and lose sight of your aims and objectives. Remember, the reason you are raising your profile is so that you are able to win support to help you continue to provide the services you were set up to provide. The way you go about promoting your organisation must take into account your service users and the objectives of your project. For example, if part of your organisation's objectives is to campaign for access for disabled people, your publicity material must be accessible – ideally, it should be available in a variety of forms, e.g. Braille or tape, etc. Or if you are an organisation working towards equal rights for women, you would need to ensure that your publicity avoided the use of stereotyping.

However, some organisations find that stereotyped images of their service users are the best way of attracting support. It is up to the organisation to discuss and agree the right approach, balancing the short-term benefits of extra funds against the possible long-term damage to the way people who use your service are perceived (see *Images: Cause or Effect?* page 33).

It is important to ensure that your profile raising work is closely linked to the rest of the activities of the organisation, otherwise you could end up compromising the principles of your organisation. Your organisation's basic philosophy needs to have a bearing not just on the way in which you provide services but also on your marketing. Consultation with your colleagues can help to clear up any grey areas.

Here are a list of things you could think about, which might help you to decide on the direction your publicity should take:

◆ Establish a set of ground rules and make sure they are agreed by everyone in the organisation

◆ Set up rules about language use

◆ Ensure there is a mechanism for a second party in the organisation who is not involved in raising your profile who can approve material.

Competing with other organisations

Another factor to consider is the possibility that you could be inadvertently competing for publicity or money with other organisations near you doing similar work. If you look as though you are stepping on their toes, you may upset them and damage your relationship with them.

One way of avoiding this is to develop a dialogue with that organisation and establish whether you could work together to organise a joint promotion which would benefit both organisations. Whilst the cause you are dealing with might be the same, there will always be

Advocates for Animals is an organisation based in Edinburgh, campaigning for animal rights and the abolition of vivisection.

The organisation maintains good links with other animal welfare organisations and avoids competition by inviting them to any public action they organise. Advocates for Animals also emphasises the fact that it is the only anti-vivisection organisation in Scotland, whilst other animal welfare organisations, which the public may consider to be undertaking the same work, actually undertake other activities. One such example is the Scottish Society for the Prevention of Cruelty to Animals. Although it too is an animal welfare organisation, its main focus is on abuse of companion animals, rather than specifically on the abolition of vivisection.

differences between the two organisations which make each unique and worth supporting (e.g. one organisation may operate within a particular geographical remit and the other within another; one organisation might provide counselling services specifically for women, the other might provide the same services but aimed at young people).

Collaboration can be turned into a positive virtue. People believe that there are too many charities and too many agencies all doing the same thing. Collaboration shows that you have thought about this too, and that you are operating efficiently and cost-effectively with each partner bringing their own particular talents and strengths to bear on the problem.

Even if working together is not feasible, try to avoid fostering a competitive atmosphere – working in the voluntary sector is, after all, all about co-operation. Focus instead on aspects of your work which make it different from the "rival" organisation and always seek to liaise with the other organisation, so that they don't feel you are going behind their back.

KEY POINTS

- Set up a dialogue
- Establish joint initiatives where appropriate
- Focus on the differences and special features of your organisation
- Avoid fostering a competitive atmosphere

Here again are a few hints:

- Work together to promote aspects of mutual concern
- Establish and promote your differences
- Talk to each other!

Need versus funding

Another dilemma that organisations often have to face is whether they should provide those services which are more likely to attract funding, but which do not necessarily cater for the greatest need. This problem is most often encountered by those organisations seeking local government funding.

KEY POINTS

♀ If you take on a new service to meet funding criteria, make sure it falls within the aims and objectives of your organisation

♀ Think of the impact of diversifying your services on your existing services

One of the main things to remember is that your primary purpose is to meet a need. You should never put yourself in a position where your services are funding-led rather than needs-led. What is important is that, when you are looking for a grant or seeking a contract to run a service, what you are proposing is in line with the priorities of your organisation. It may be possible to incorporate the new work quite easily into your mainstream activities. For example, you could be contracted to provide counselling services for young people, where your current services offer counselling across the board. This might mean organising special session for this particular client group or promoting yourselves to attract this group of people.

Whatever you do, it is essential to look at the impact of diversification on your other services. Would providing extra services mean cutting your existing services? Would it mean reducing the management time you can spend to ensure that all your work is of a high quality? Would it be less effective than concentrating on one thing and doing it well?

You may decide that you cannot provide the services you are being asked to provide, because they are too far removed from the aims of your organisation. This was the case when certain national children's charities refused to discuss the possibility of running secure homes for young offenders, when this was suggested by the government. You might need to acknowledge that the statutory sector may no longer support your organisation and that you will have to start looking further afield for your funding (see *Broadening your funding base*, page 103).

3 Strategies

Apart from fundraising and promotion there are a few additional strategies that "hard-to-sell" organisations might find helpful.

You are a part of the voluntary sector

It is always as well to be aware of the fact that you are a part of the wider "voluntary sector". The "voluntary sector", as an entity consists not just of voluntary groups like yourselves, but also of a whole range of support and information networks set up for charities and voluntary organisations to tap into.

There are advice agencies around the country like local Councils of Voluntary Service, Rural Community Councils and Charities Information Bureaux, which can offer information on charitable status, fundraising and other matters. National organisations such as the National Council for Voluntary Organisations (NCVO), the Scottish Council for Voluntary Organisations, Northern Ireland Council for Voluntary Action and Wales Council for Voluntary Action can provide support and backup for voluntary organisations on a range of areas and may be able to offer advice on fundraising.

There are also much more specialist networks relating to particular fields of interest. For example, there are umbrella groups like the National Alliance of Women's Organisations, Sia (for black and ethnic minority organisations) and the British Council of Organisations of Disabled People which can give you specialist information and can provide useful contacts.

Additionally, there are a range of different organisations providing very specific services for voluntary organisations, for example the Institute of Charity Fundraising Managers runs conferences and training, BITC (Business in the Community) provides information about corporate involvement with voluntary groups and secondments. (See *Useful Organisations*, page 109.)

Another way of getting access to information is through establishing networks with other organisations working in your field. This not only promotes good relations, but also encourages mutual support and sharing of ideas and often prevents you from having to "reinvent the wheel". Many people are prepared to share their ideas with you and will benefit just as much in return.

Never underestimate the wealth of support, information and resources that you can access just by being a voluntary organisation. Being aware of all the sources of help that are available to you and tapping into them can make your life a lot easier.

KEY POINTS

- Know your networks
- Make the most of the support and resources that networks can bring you

---

The **Black HIV/AIDS Forum** (BHAF), an organisation based in Leicester, provides a range of services around HIV and AIDS for Asian, African and African-Caribbean people. It also campaigns to highlight the need for services for Black communities.

BHAF has found it most useful to network with other Black organisations and HIV/AIDS groups. Kala Chauhan, Outreach and Development Coordinator, has established a wide network of contacts with people working in the voluntary sector. The exchange of information and support that has resulted from this network has meant that it is not just BHAF that benefits, but everyone that participates.

✍ Networking to promote your cause

by Vijay Krishnarayan, Environment Support Team, NCVO

Despite current over-use of the term networking, the concept has much to commend itself to groups which have traditionally found themselves denied access to ever-decreasing resources. It can be turned to good use as a powerful tool that can open up previously closed doors and considerably strengthen groups that participate, particularly those which want to raise their profile and thereby enhance their prospects of raising much needed funds.

"Super Networker" is fast becoming a caricature. A super hero character borne of the 80s, this filofaxing individual always hits the ground running, attending conferences and receptions in order to make dates, to "do lunch" with people. Super Networker never chatted to people – she touched base with them – all in an attempt to accrue more business contacts, information or anything else that could help progress her career. Much as any of us would shudder to think of ourselves as being typified as a Super Networker, there are things we can learn from her virtues and shortcomings.

But first let us look at what we mean when we talk about a network. A network provides the framework for groups and individuals to come together with a defined purpose. With that common concern in mind, partners from an array of backgrounds can go on to share information, expertise and other resources. These in turn can be harnessed by partici-pants in the network to promote their own efforts. Networks are not another layer of bureaucracy that place a drain on its constituent parts. They are a method of improving the way that we work with each other and relate to organisations outside the voluntary sector.

Networking can exist at a number of different levels. One of the most frequently heard criticisms of networking is that people have been talking to each other for years and no one ever needed to give it a fancy name before. To a certain extent networking can amount to talking to each other, for example, at a party, but that is an extremely limited view of what networking involves. Increasingly, groups are joining formal networks recognising the value of affiliating to a structure that can prove very useful.

There are a number of different networks that have become an established feature of the voluntary sector. Local development agencies (LDAs) provide generic support to a wide range of local bodies whose only common thread is that they are voluntary groups. Whether the LDA is a Council for Voluntary Service, Rural Community Council or Volunteer Bureau, they can all provide advice on fundraising issues and contacts in the local authority and broker new relationships between organisations.

There are also national umbrella organisations that provide support and advice to groups working in a particular field, for example in care or development. In addition to these some of the larger national bodies now see themselves as federations of local agencies. With resources scarce, some national bodies have joined forces with other organisations in order to deliver services, launch appeals or mount campaigns.

To find out more about the array of networks that exist a good starting point would be the nearest LDA (see *Useful Organisations*, page 109). Otherwise there are many directories that list the growing number of specialist sector networks. If there is no LDA in your area, then these directories (see *Useful Publications*, page 119) should be available at local libraries.

But before a group considers entering a formal network, the fundamental question it should ask itself is "What do we actually need?". After all, it is very rare for people to affiliate to a network on the basis of altruism – inevitably something is sought in return for a subscription fee or for time given up in attending meetings. But at the same time it is rare for a network to guarantee access to a pot of gold. What groups should be doing is looking at what is needed in order to get access to that pot of gold. Is the information provided in a newsletter from a network capable of being used to inform a funding bid or to provide background information on what others have tried or on what current trends are? On a national level for example, training on marketing can be accessed through one network such as the National Association of Councils for Voluntary Service, which runs a national network of training centres, offering short courses programmes.

If there isn't a network that meets a group's requirements then it might be worth considering setting up one of its own. This self-help approach does not require a wealth of resources. For example, it does not take a vast amount of staff time and there is nothing compelling groups to physically meet with other members of the network. A network might connect groups working in a particular field or looking for solutions to a particular problem. It could operate on the barest minimum effort, enabling like-minded organisations to exchange information and improve their working practices. However, a network must recognise that if there is insufficient commitment or when particular objectives have been reached, it is time either to call the network to a halt or to review its work. Networking is a means to an end, rather than an end in itself.

All of this may be well and good when information on potential partners is available, but sometimes groups can come up against a brick wall. Voluntary organisations often cite statutory bodies as being impervious to approaches for information. In order to network best in these circumstances, a group should use any existing contacts to help establish new contacts. If no contacts exist then groups should get in touch with other organisations who might be able to help. This information can be as precious as any other resource if it allows a group to collect important information on potential funders, their procedures and practices.

So, are there any examples of networks that deliver services which enhance a group's performance? Formal networks have been set up to encourage and support organisations that want to get involved in environmental work. The North East Environment Network has produced an authoritative directory of regional contacts. The Merseyside Environment Trust coordinates events in the area during Environment Week, giving small grants to groups. Other networks provide a mailing service featuring the work of one or more of their members. All of these functions promote the constituent parts rather than the network itself. The services that they provide succeed in drawing attention to the activities or needs of individual groups.

Groups that are affiliated to these environment networks have not necessarily joined with the specific aim of enhancing their fundraising prospects. However, by joining they have gained access to a wide range of information, expertise and support, all of which helps them function more effectively and in turn may well make them more attractive to potential funders.

The key to successful networking is openness. If a group wants information from others it has to be prepared to give something in return. This may be a fee or a service, but equally, it could be other kinds of information that might be highly prized by another group. An open approach should extend to all areas of a group's work, for example, inviting others to come and see the work that is being done at a particular project. Funders will be impressed by open days and events that expose projects they could be associated with to a wider audience. In addition, some funders network amongst themselves so they will soon get to hear of examples of good and bad practice.

Meanwhile over a breakfast meeting Super Networker plies her trade making ever more contacts. Her go-for-it attitude brushes aside any trace of self doubt. A good lesson for groups who should be confident of their own abilities if they are going to convince others that they are worth supporting. Super Networker has total belief in herself. But all that activity does leave you wondering if she ever leaves herself any time to put all this information to any use – beware of networking for networking's sake.

There is no need for staff (paid or voluntary) or management committees of groups to turn themselves into Super Networker. However, there is nothing wrong with identifying an objective and seeing who or what will enable a group to achieve what might seem to be out of reach. With the number of groups growing and the resources available shrinking, groups are increasingly having to think laterally and employ new techniques to reach their goals. Networking can help, if you know what you are looking for.

Planning ahead

Sometimes small organisations are very good at mobilising commitment and enthusiasm, but not so good at thinking about the future survival of the organisation. An organisation cannot function without the firm commitment of those working within it, but neither can it survive without agreeing about how the organisation's work will develop and making plans to facilitate this development. Even if you are not intending to expand the work of your organisation, you will still need to think carefully about how you will continue to provide the services you are currently providing. Planning ahead means looking at how needs are changing and at how services to meet these needs are developing. It means deciding how your projects will expand and develop in the future, and looking at where your organisation plans to go. Planning ahead also involves looking at what others are doing – both in the voluntary and the statutory sectors – and at the sorts of partnerships you should be developing with them. If you are going to secure long-term funding for these services, again you will have to think ahead.

This doesn't just mean planning the odd fundraising event every now and then; it involves thinking much more broadly than this. You should try to develop relationships with potential funders well before you begin to ask them for support. Enhancing your public profile goes hand in hand with your fundraising strategy and is an investment in your future. Planning a promotional strategy and putting it into action are vital elements in any organisation's efforts to survive.

A good fundraising strategy (see *Developing a fundraising strategy*, page 70) combined with a plan to promote the name and work of your organisation and the importance of the needs you are addressing will help secure the well-being of the organisation, now and in the future.

Defining the role of your management committee

The management committee of any organisation can contribute towards the well-being and smooth running of the organisation. However, if the roles and responsibilities of the members of the management committee are not clearly laid out from the outset, there can be misunderstandings and an imbalance in the division of the workload.

It is not unusual for a management committee to be comprised of volunteers who have other commitments. What is important is that members of the committee know in advance what is expected of them. A job description is a good idea and can help to outline the role and responsibilities of each member of the committee. It can also enable people to look realistically at the amount of time they can commit to the organisation.

The **Fellowship of Depressives Anonymous** is a self-help organisation in North Humberside for people who suffer from depression. It provides information on depression and encourages the formation of local groups.

The management committee is comprised entirely of volunteers. Regular bi-monthly meetings are held so that the committee can feed back information. All members of the management committee have detailed job descriptions outlining each person's responsibilities and day-to-day duties. Most of the organisation's activities, such as publishing a newsletter and answering queries, are undertaken by members of the management committee, although other activities, such as the fellowship's penfriend scheme are run by non-members.

Apart from running most of the activities of the organisation, members of the management committee also have some influential contacts who can help raise the profile of the organisation.

Members of staff also need to have a degree of input into the agreement and both staff and management committee should be clear about each other's role. This means there must be effective communication between the two.

There are a number of functions that members of the management committee are obliged to take on. This includes their legal responsibilities, managing the organisation's finances and property, and making the organisation accountable; and their supervisory and strategic role, which involves giving the organisation direction. However, the committee can also function as a useful resource for the organisation – its members might be able to provide useful contacts for the organisation, help reinforce donor relations and promote the organisation, or act as volunteers to help get the work done (which is different from their other role of ensuring that it is done).

Broadening your funding base

Many small organisations, having relied on statutory sources of funding for their core costs have only just begun to explore the possibility of funding from grant-making trusts and companies. Although trusts and companies are easy to identify, they are constantly being approached by fundraisers. Contacts, skill, persistence and luck are all important elements of a successful application. However, it may also be beneficial to develop individual support through subscriptions and donations or from fundraising events.

Another area to consider is selling goods to generate a profit for your work. If you do this there are two things to remember: first, it is usually easier to ask for money than it is to earn it; and second, if the trading falls outside your organisation's primary purpose, you may

KEY POINTS

- Don't rely on statutory funding
- Think about new ways of raising money

need to set up a trading arm as a vehicle for the trading activity. You should seek legal advice if you intend to do this.

Some of the most popular ways to raise money commercially include setting up charity shops and producing gift catalogues. Organisations such as Oxfam, Greenpeace and Save the Children all undertake trading on this scale. But, a word of warning: these activities often fail to get that much of a return and may be too ambitious for many smaller organisations. It may be more appropriate to look into trading at a local level on a more modest scale. For example, you could run a stall at a local festival or other event or produce goods to sell, such as greetings cards, T-shirts and badges. These activities can contribute to raising awareness of your cause and top up your income.

CASE STUDY

The Naz Project

The Naz Project is an initiative providing different types of support for people with HIV or AIDS from the South Asian, Turkish, Iranian and Arab communities based in West London. The project's services include advice lines in eight different languages, counselling and befriending schemes.

Shivananda Khan, founder of the project, maintains that there is no equivalent gay consciousness within the Asian community, which has proven so strong in the development of HIV/AIDS services elsewhere and that "the family" and ideas of caste take precedence over social awareness. This makes appealing to the Asian community much more difficult. Funders, lacking an awareness of the specific needs of Asian people with HIV or AIDS, often fail to target their funding.

The Naz Project has responded to these difficulties by acknowledging the strong notions of tradition and the family within the South Asian, Turkish, Iranian and Arab communities and by using family networks as part of its fundraising strategy. This approach not only wins financial support, but also helps raise awareness of HIV/AIDS issues amongst the community that Naz aims to serve. Khan hopes that by tapping into his own community, the project will be able to free itself from the uncertainties of statutory funding. Indeed, whilst the project received a considerable amount of statutory funding (both from central and local government) in the early days, Khan believes that the services Naz provides do not always match the requirements of contract funding, e.g. as calls are made on an anonymous basis, in line with Naz's confidentiality policy, it is impossible to give funders acceptable data on clients.

The project is therefore looking towards Asian businesses and wealthy Asian individuals for support as a solution to the vagaries of statutory funding. These Khan will come by through personal contacts ("mainly through friends of friends of friends"). Asian film stars are another large untouched area of potential support.

Additionally, the Naz Project is planning to extend its trading arm with the aim of supplementing income through the production and sale of various materials. Awareness tapes in a number of different Asian languages are a cheap resource for overseas projects and discussions are taking place regarding the possibility of franchising some products to India.

/ **CASE STUDY** \

Prisoners Abroad

Prisoners Abroad (PA) was set up in 1978 as a support service for prisoners in countries outside the UK and their families. The public commonly perceives the organisation as representing people who have committed a crime and who are therefore not a worthy cause.

The organisation has a budget of £300,000. £70,000 comes from the Home Office, £40,000 from the London Boroughs Grants Committee and £130,000 from charitable trusts. The remainder comes from 3,000 individual donors (£50,000) and occasional fundraising events. Between £3,000 and £5,000 is donated by companies.

Where funding is concerned, it is often difficult for PA to meet a number of trusts's geographical criteria, as much of the organisation's work takes place abroad. This has been overcome by identifying aspects of the organisation's work which do match these trusts's criteria, e.g., PA has approached those trusts specifying an interest in education for support for education projects for prisoners. Where individual donors are concerned, it is a matter of convincing people that the work is worthy of support. Companies, however, are the most difficult area to gain support from. It is not easy for an organisation like PA to offer a company something tangible in return for its support. But it is not impossible. PA is looking at ways of tapping into the corporate funding pot and arranged a corporate dinner at Lloyds, sponsored by a range of companies at which the Foreign Secretary spoke.

With only two fundraisers, PA prefers to pursue avenues of support that are likely to be fruitful. Volunteers, however, can help to find out about the less obvious areas of support, by establishing a database of captains of industry, to whom Ian Richter, a well known ex-prisoner, has written, which raised significant new corporate income. The database is now being sold to other charities and has so far raised in excess of £40,000 for the voluntary sector.

The organisation's publicity is done through reciprocal mailings, inserts in publications with a sympathetic readership and letters to the press. Publicity concerning the plight of hostages has contributed to greater public concern and understanding and journalists now often approach PA directly if there is likely to be a human interest story.

The organisation also participates in the Penal Affairs Consortium and is establishing an international network of similar organisations. This opportunity for information exchange further enhances the organisation's profile and reinforces its credibility. Additionally, PA involves itself at governmental level, suggesting changes in the Criminal Justice Bill and putting forward ideas for the distribution of the lottery funds.

Summing Up

Image-building and fundraising are part and parcel of a successful and effective voluntary organisation. How much of these activities you undertake and what techniques you use will depend on the way your organisation works and the level of resources you have. Use every opportunity you get to demonstrate that you are an effective and efficient organisation and a cause worth supporting. Think carefully about the people you were set up for or the cause you are working for and about how your publicity and fundraising strategies fit in around them.

Here is a short recap:

When considering image-building...

♦ Whom do you want to reach?

♦ Which medium will best reach these people?

♦ What can you do to improve your relationship with your supporters?

♦ How can you improve the presentation of your publicity materials?

♦ What do your name and logo say about you?

When considering fundraising...

♦ Is your fundraising strategy realistic?

♦ Does your funding approach go beyond statutory sources?

♦ How can your project proposal be adapted to meet the criteria of a funder, which does not specify a policy to support your field

♦ Is your costing realistic – does it take all aspects of your project into account?

♦ How well do you keep funders informed?

Promotion and fundraising need not be as daunting as they sound and they don't have to mean "selling out", "buying into the establishment" or even "behaving like business". If you put in a lot of thought and keep the aims and objectives of your organisation in sight, you can come up with some exciting initiatives that could seriously benefit your cause long-term.

Useful Organisations

*This section is not intended as an exhaustive list of organi-
sations, but simply as a guide for voluntary organisations
to the kinds of networks that can be tapped into.*

Alcohol and Drug Use

Northern Ireland Regional Drugs Unit
Shaftesbury Hospital, 116-122 Great Victoria Street,
Belfast, BT2 7BG
tel. 0232-329808

Scottish Drug Forum
5 Oswald Street, Glasgow, G1 5QR
tel. 041-221 1175

Standing Conference on Drug Abuse
1-4 Hatton Place, Hatton Garden, London, EC1N 8ND
tel. 071-430 2341
(England and Wales)

Business/Management/
Secondments of company staff

Action Resource Centre (ARC)
8 Stratton Street, London, W1X 5FD
tel. 071- 629 2209
(England, Wales and Scotland)

Action Resource Centre Northern Ireland
103-107 York Street, Belfast, BT15 1AB
tel. 0232-328000

Business in the Community
8 Stratton Street, London W1X 5FD
tel. 071- 629 1600
(England, Wales and Northern Ireland)

Scottish Business in the Community
Romana House, 43 Station Road, Corstorphine,
Edinburgh, EH12 7AF
tel. 031-334 9876

Community issues

Community Development Foundation
60 Highbury Grove, London, N5 2AG
tel. 071-226 5375
(England, Wales, Scotland and Northern Ireland)

**National Association of Councils for
Voluntary Service (NACVS)**
3rd Floor, Arundel Court, 177 Arundel Street,
Sheffield, S1 2NU
tel. 0742 786636
(England)

Disability issues

British Council of Organisations of Disabled People
De Bradelei House, Chapel Street, Belper, Derby, DE56 1AR
tel. 0773-828182
(England, Wales, Scotland)

Disarmament

National Peace Council
88 Islington High Street, London, N1 8EG
tel. 071-354 5200
(England, Wales, Scotland and Northern Ireland)

Ethnic minority issues

Chinese Information and Advice Centre
68 Shaftesbury Avenue, London, W1V 7DF
tel. 071-836 8291
(London-based, but enquiries taken from England,
Wales, Scotland and Northern Ireland)

Commission for Racial Equality
Elliott House, 10-12 Allington Street, London, SW1E 5EH
tel. 071-828 7022
(England, Wales, Scotland, Northern Ireland)

Confederation of Indian Organisations (UK)
170 Tolcarne Drive, Pinner, Middlesex, HA5 2DR
tel. 081-863 9089
(England, Wales, Scotland and Northern Ireland)

Cypriot Advisory Service
26 Crowndale Road, London, NW1 1TT
tel. 071-387 6617
(England, Wales, Scotland, Northern Ireland)

Sia
49-51 Bedford Row, London, WC1V 6DJ
tel. 071-430 0811
(England, Wales, Scotland)

**Standing Conference of West Indian
Organisations in Great Britain**
5 Westminster Bridge Road, London, SE1 7XW
tel. 071-928 7861
(England and Wales)

Union of Muslim Organisations of UK and Eire
109 Campden Hill Road, London, W8 7TL
tel. 071-229 0538
(England, Wales, Scotland and Northern Ireland)

Fundraising

Charity Projects
74 New Oxford Street, London, WC1A 1EF
tel. 071-436 1122
(England, Wales, Scotland and Northern Ireland)

Directory of Social Change
Radius Works, Back Lane, London, NW3 1HL
tel. 071-435 8171

3rd Floor, Federation House, Hope Street, Liverpool, L1 9BW
tel. 051-708 0117

(England, Wales, Scotland and Northern Ireland)

Institute of Charity Fundraising Managers
208-210 Market Towers, 1 Nine Elms Lane, London, SW8 5NQ
tel. 071- 627 3436
(England and Wales)

Institute of Charity Fundraising Managers in Scotland
c/o Penumbra, Gogar Park, 167 Glasgow Road,
Edinburgh, EH12 9BG
tel. 031-317 1337
(Scotland)

HIV/AIDS

National AIDS Trust
6th Floor, Eileen House, 80 Newington Causeway,
London, SE1 6EF
tel. 071-972 2845
(England, Wales, Scotland and Northern Ireland)

Homelessness

Federation of Black Housing Organisations
374 Gray's Inn Road, London, WC1X 8BB
tel. 071-837 8288
(England, Wales, Scotland and Northern Ireland)

National Federation of Housing Associations
175 Gray's Inn Road, London WC1X 8UP
tel. 071-278 6571
(England)

National Association of Voluntary Hostels
Fulham Palace, Bishops Avenue, London, SW6 6EA
tel. 071-731 4205
(England, Wales, Scotland and Northern Ireland)

Northern Ireland Federation of Housing Associations
Carlisle Memorial Centre, 88 Clifton Street, Belfast, BT13
tel. 0232 230446

Scottish Federation of Housing Associations
38 York Place, Edinburgh, EH1 3HU
tel. 031-556 5777

Welsh Federation of Housing Associations
Norbury House, Norbury Road, Fairwater, Cardiff, CF5 3AS
tel. 0222 555022

Human Rights

Committee for the Administration of Justice
45-47 Donegall Street, Belfast, BT1 2FG
tel. 0232 232394
(Northern Ireland)

Liberty – National Council for Civil Liberties
21 Tabard Street, London, SE1 4LA
tel. 071-403 3888
(England, Wales and Northern Ireland)

Minority Rights Group Ltd.
379 Brixton Road, London, SW9 7DE
tel. 071-978 9498
(England, Wales, Scotland and Northern Ireland)

Scottish Council for Civil Liberties
146 Holland Street, Glasgow, G2 4NG
tel. 041-332 5960

Lesbian and Gay Issues

London Lesbian and Gay Switchboard
BM Switchboard, London, WC1N 3XX
tel. 071-837 7324
(Referrals to local switchboards across England,
Wales, Scotland and Northern Ireland)

Lesbian and Gay Employment Rights (LAGER)
St Margaret's House, 21 Old Ford Road, Globetown, Bethnal
Green, London E2 9PL
tel. 081-983 0696
(England, Wales, Scotland and Northern Ireland)

Stonewall Lobby Group Ltd.
2 Greycoat Place, London, SW1P 1SB
tel. 071-222 9007
(England, Wales, Scotland and Northern Ireland)

Mental Health

Mental Health Foundation
37 Mortimer Street, London, W1N 7RT
tel. 071-580 0145
(England, Wales, Scotland, Northern Ireland)

Offenders

**National Association for the Care and
Resettlement of Offenders (NACRO)**
169 Clapham Road, London, SW9 0PU
tel. 071-582 6500
(England and Wales)

**Northern Ireland Association for the Care and
Resettlement of Offenders (NIACRO)**
169 Ormeau Road, Belfast, BT7 1SQ
tel. 0232 320157

**Scottish Association for the Care and
Resettlement of Offenders (SIACRO)**
31 Palmerston Place, Edinburgh, EH12 5AP
tel. 031-226 4222

Registering as a charity/applying
for tax concessions

Charity Commission
St Alban's House, 57-60 Haymarket, London, SW1Y 4QX
tel. 071-210 3000

Graeme House, Derby Square, Liverpool, L2 7SB
tel. 051-227 3191

Woodfield House, Tangier, Taunton, Somerset, TA1 4BL
tel. 0823 345000

(England and Wales)

Inland Revenue Claims Branch, Charity Division
St John's House, Merton Road, Bootle, Merseyside, L69 9BB
tel. 051-472 6000
(Northern Ireland)

Inland Revenue Claims Scotland
Trinity Park House, South Trinity Road, Edinburgh, EH5 3SD
tel. 031-551 8127
(Scotland)

Rural issues

Action with Communities in Rural England (ACRE)
Somerford Court, Somerford Road, Cirencester,
Gloucester, GL7 1TW
tel. 0285-653477

Highland and Islands Enterprise
Bridge House, 20 Bridge Street, Inverness, IV1 1QR
tel. 0463 234171

Rural Community Network Northern Ireland
4 Molesworth Street, Cookstown, County Tyrone, BT80 8NX
tel. 064 8766670

Rural Development Commission
11 Cowley Street, London, SW1P 3NA
tel. 071-276 6969
(England)

Rural Development Council for Northern Ireland
Loughry College, Cookstown, County Tyrone, BT80 9AA
tel. 06487 66980

Rural Forum
Highland House, St Catherine's Road, Perth, PH1 5RY
tel. 0738 34565
(Scotland)

Welsh Development Agency
Pearl House, Greyfriars Road, Cardiff, CF1 3XX
tel. 0222 222666

Voluntary sector development

Charities Aid Foundation
48 Pembury Road, Tonbridge, Kent, TN9 2JD
tel. 0732 771333
(England, Wales, Scotland and Northern Ireland)

Federation of Independent Advice Centres
Concourse House, Lime Street, Liverpool, L1 1NY
tel. 071-274 1839
(England, Wales, Scotland and Northern Ireland)

National Council for Voluntary Organisations
Regents Wharf, 8 All Saints Street, London, N1 9RL
tel. 071-713 6161
(England)

Community Matters (National Federation of Community Organisations)
8-9 Upper Street, London, N1 0PQ
tel. 071-226 0189
(England, Wales, Scotland and Northern Ireland)

Northern Ireland Council of Voluntary Action
127 Ormeau Road, Belfast, BT7 1SH
tel. 0232 321224

Scottish Council for Voluntary Organisations
18-19 Claremont Crescent, Edinburgh, EH7 4QD
tel. 031-556 3882

Wales Council for Voluntary Action
Llys Ifor, Heol Crescent, Caerffili, Canol Morgannwg, CF8 1XL
tel. 0222 869224/5/6 or 0222-869111

Volunteering

Northern Ireland Volunteer Development Agency
Annsgate House, 70-74 Ann Street, Belfast, BT1 4EH
tel. 0232 236100

Resource Unit to Promote Black Volunteering
First Floor, 102 Park Village East, London, NW1 3SP
tel. 071-388 8542
(England, Wales, Scotland and Northern Ireland)

Volunteer Centre UK
29 Lower Kings Road, Berkhamsted, Herts, HP4 2AB
tel. 04427 73311
(England)

Volunteer Development Scotland
80 Murray Place, Stirling, SK8 2BX
tel. 0786 479593

Wales Council for Voluntary Action
(see Voluntary sector development above for address/tel. above)

Women's issues

Equal Opportunities Commission
(Voluntary Organisations Liaison Unit)
Overseas House, Quay Street, Manchester, M3 3HN
tel. 061-833 9244
(England, Wales and Scotland)

Equal Opportunities Commission for Northern Ireland
Chamber of Commerce House, 22 Great Victoria Street,
Belfast, BT2 7BA
tel. 0232 242752

National Alliance of Women's Organisations
279/281 Whitechapel Road, London, E1 1BY
tel. 071-247 7052
(England)

Northern Ireland Federation of Townswomen's Guilds
18 Jellicoe Avenue, Belfast, BT15 3FZ

Wales Assembly of Women
Dyffryn Esplanade, Carmarthen, Dyfed
tel. 0267 236188

Women's Forum Scotland
5a Crown Circus, Glasgow, G12 9HB
tel. 041 332 7321

Women's National Commission
Caxton House, Tothill Street, London SW1H 9NF
tel. 071-273 5486
(England, Wales, Scotland and Northern Ireland)

Useful Publications

This section lists publications which organisations may find useful. It is not an exhaustive list.

Fundraising

The AIDS Funding Manual, Resourcing the HIV/AIDS Voluntary Sector in London, published by the Directory of Social Change (DSC), Radius Works, Back Lane, London, NW3 1HL, £6.95 (plus £1.50 p & p).

The Arts Funding Guide 1994, published by DSC (see address above), £14.95 (plus £1.50 p & p).

Central Government Grants Guide, published by DSC (see address above), £12.95 (plus £1.50 p & p).

The Complete Fundraising Handbook, published by DSC (see address above), £9.95 (plus £1.50 p & p).

Directory of Grant-Making Trusts, published by Charities Aid Foundation (CAF), 48 Pembury Road, Tonbridge, Kent, TN9 2JD, £50 (plus £3.80 p & p).

Environmental Grants, A Guide to Grants for the Environment from Government, Companies and Charitable Trusts, published by DSC (see address above), £14.95 (plus £1.50 p & p).

Guide for the Voluntary Sector to the Scottish Office Grants, free copies available from Cathy Douglas, tel. 031-244 5550.

Guide to Company Giving 1993, published by DSC (see address above), £14.95 (plus £1.50 p & p).

Guide to the Major Trusts 1993, Volumes 1 & 2, published by DSC (see address above), £14.95 each (plus £1.50 p & p).

HIV/AIDS: A Funding Guide for England and Wales – Grants for HIV Projects Outside London, published by DSC (see address above), £7.95 (plus £1.50 p & p).

Irish Funding Handbook, published by Creative Activity for Everyone (CAFE), The City Centre, 23-25 Moss Street, Dublin 2, Republic of Ireland (also available from DSC, see address above), £10 (plus £1.50 p & p).

London Grants Guide, published by DSC (see address above), £12.50 (plus £1.50 p & p).

Major Companies Guide 1994, published by DSC (see address above), £14.95 (plus £1.50 p & p).

Resourcing the Voluntary Sector: The Funders' Perspective, published by the Association of Charitable Foundations, High Holborn House, 52-54 High Holborn, London, WC1V 6RL, £9 (includes p & p).

Wales Funding Handbook/Llawlyfrcyllido Cymru, 1992/93, published by Wales Council for Voluntary Action, Llys Ifor, Crescent Road, Caerphilly, Mid Glamorgan, CF8 1XL, £5 (includes p & p).

West Midlands Grants Guide, published by DSC (see address above), £9.95 (plus £1.50 p & p).

Women's Guide to the European Social Fund, published by the National Alliance of Women's Organisations, 279/281 Whitechapel Road, London, E1 1BY, £1.50 (including p & p).

Writing Better Fundraising Applications, published by DSC (see address above), £9.95 (plus p & p).

Contract Culture

Contracts in Practice, published by DSC (see address above) and NCVO, Regents Wharf, 8 All Saints Street, London, N1 9RL, £8.95 (plus £1.50 p & p).

Costing for Contracts, published by DSC and NCVO (see addresses above), £8.95 (plus £1.50 p & p).

From Grants to Contracts, published by DSC and NCVO (see addresses above), £8.95 (plus £1.50 p & p).

Getting Ready for Contracts, published by DSC (see address above), £8.95 (plus £1.50 p & p).

Volunteering

Making the Most of Employee Community Involvement, published by the Volunteer Centre UK, 29 Lower Kings Road, Berkhamsted, Herts, HP4 2AB, £4 (including p & p).

Miscellaneous

The Campaigning Handbook, published by DSC (see address above), £9.95 (plus p & p).

Chasing the EC Rainbow: Women in Northern Ireland and the Impact of European Community Funding, published by the Irish Congress of Trade Unions Women's Committee, Irish Congress of Trade Unions, 3 Wellington Park, Belfast, BT9, £2 (including p & p).

Organising Local Events, published by DSC (see address above), £7.95 (plus p & p).

Rural Action: A collection of Community Work Case Studies, published by Pluto Press, 345 Archway Road, London, N6 5AA, £14.20 (including p & p).

The Voluntary Agencies Directory, published by the NCVO (see address above), £12.95.

Notes